You *must* read this book. Too many people around you are grieving hard yet are clueless as to how to fill the emptiness. Be warned: This impossibly personal work treads on delicate territory (Who among us is an expert in helping the anguished deal well with loss?). Take heart, though; you have a seasoned, skilled guide in Nancy Guthrie. She has ingested the bitter bread of loss, which makes her counsel wise, wonderful, and best of all, *authentic*. In *God Does His Best Work with Empty*, my treasured friend shares insights that are grounded in Scripture and filled with tested-and-tried-compassion. Best of all, she knows Jesus well and understands how to gently point hurting people his way. So read it. And let its wisdom push you out into a hurting world where only Christ can fill those who are empty.

JONI EARECKSON TADA, Joni and Friends International Disability Center

Nancy's writing is like a familiar pair of hands tenderly taking hold of our faces and an empathetic set of eyes, locking with ours to remind us of what has never stopped being true. Her words do the important work of acknowledging our ache, then lifting our gaze to the cross and the hope of eternity it secures for us. This book does that work patiently, thoughtfully, and expertly.

RAECHEL MYERS, cofounder of She Reads Truth

Nancy Guthrie is one of my favorite writers, not least of all because she's saturated with God's Word. She affirms Jesus without ever offering cheap "get-on-with-it" advice that is code for "stop grieving, it makes us uncomfortable." With honesty and transparency, Nancy affirms gospel truth that encourages, corrects, and empowers us to embrace the blood-bought goodness and joy of Jesus. This is a terrific book.

RANDY ALCORN, author of *Heaven, If God is Good,* and *Giving Is the Good Life*

Nancy Guthrie is always a source of sound wisdom for me, and *God Does His Best Work with Empty* is no different. Offering deep sympathy and life-giving hope, this book will strengthen your heart in the weary places and point you to the joy and promise of being filled by Christ.

LAURA WIFLER, cofounder of Risen Motherhood; podcaster; coauthor of *Risen Motherhood: Gospel Hope for Everyday Moments*

I noticed while reading through the Bible one year that God frequently used women's barren, empty wombs to bring timely deliverance to his people. After reading this book, I now know why: God does his best work with empty vessels! In a world of clichés and pat answers to real problems, Nancy Guthrie speaks divine truth, explaining not only *why* God uses emptiness but *how.* Finally—a Scripture-based explanation that causes me first to think, then to worship our ever-filling God! The prayer at the conclusion of the book is something I personally plan to incorporate in my own journey moving forward. We all experience *empty* somewhere in our lives, and this book has helped me know how to fill it. Thank you, thank you for this biblical solution to emptiness!

DAVID ARTHUR, CEO and President, Precept Ministries

We all want to be skilled in connecting what we feel with what God says. We certainly can feel empty; the challenge is to hear God speak in Scripture to this emptiness and to hear him speak often, with characteristic gentleness and the element of surprise and newness. Nancy is, I think, the perfect person to make those connections for us.

ED WELCH, counselor and senior faculty, CCEF

Empty is a feeling we all experience in life. When the well runs dry, how we fill it up makes all the difference in the world. Some turn to alcohol, drugs, and personal ambition to numb the pain of loss and despair. But none of those provide us with what we need most—a *real* solution. In this book you won't find sugary platitudes or shallow pick-me-ups. You will find answers and see what we've all come to expect from Nancy Guthrie. She can relate to you, she can understand you, and she can help you. In your greatest pain, you can find a greater purpose.

COSTI W. HINN, pastor and author of *God, Greed, and the (Prosperity) Gospel*

God Does His Best Work with Empty

God

does

his

best work

with

empty

NANCY
GUTHRIE

TYNDALE
MOMENTUM®

The Tyndale nonfiction imprint

Visit Tyndale online at tyndale.com.

Visit Tyndale Momentum online at tyndalemomentum.com.

TYNDALE, Tyndale Momentum, and Tyndale's quill logo are registered trademarks of Tyndale House Publishers. The Tyndale Momentum logo is a trademark of Tyndale House Publishers. Tyndale Momentum is the nonfiction imprint of Tyndale House Publishers, Carol Stream, Illinois.

God Does His Best Work with Empty

Designed by Ron C. Kaufmann

For information about special discounts for bulk purchases, please contact Tyndale House Publishers at csresponse@tyndale.com, or call 1-800-323-9400.

ISBN 978-1-4964-3969-7

Printed in China

26	25	24	23	22	21
8	7	6	5	4	3

I fondly dedicate this book to the hundreds of bereaved parents who have spent a weekend with my husband, David, and me at Respite Retreat. As we've sat in that sacred circle, I've looked into your eyes, acknowledged the emptiness in your homes and in your hearts, and assured you that God does his best work with empty.

I know the empty place is still there. There's an empty place in your family photo, an empty place at the table, an empty place in the plans you had for your future.

I'm praying that God will continue to do his best work, not in spite of your emptiness, but in it and through it.

I'm praying that God will fill your lives with his
life and light,
beauty and purpose,
hope and joy.

TABLE OF CONTENTS

INTRODUCTION

"THAT'S ME! That's my life. I feel so empty," my friend Julie said when I told her the title of the book I was working on, the book you now hold in your hands. She and her husband, both newly retired, their children far away, were struggling to figure out how to fill not just the hours in the day but the holes in their hearts. But her response to the title wasn't unique. Whenever I told people what I was working on, the most common response was a knowing, low-pitched "Mmmm."

The reality of emptiness seems to resonate.

I know it resonates with me. And I'm somewhat embarrassed to admit it because my life has been and is now filled with so much goodness. I have a multitude of reasons to be perfectly happy and completely satisfied. And yet . . .

I have often found myself fighting off a sense of

emptiness, or perhaps more accurately, wallowing in a wave of emptiness. Sometimes I feel as if there is a bottomless pit inside of me that no amount of entertainment, affirmation, or accumulation can fill. I'm ashamed of how envious I can be of what someone else has or does when I have so much and get to do so much. I've often wondered how I can feel empty immediately after accomplishing something I've worked hard for or while I'm still on the vacation I've dreamed of. I've wondered how I can feel lonely in a room full of interesting people or in a marriage to a wonderful man. I've wondered how it is that I can so quickly descend from thrilling satisfaction into nagging dissatisfaction after an expensive purchase, a successful event, or a sought-after experience.

But I do.

Of course, nothing has led to a profound sense of emptiness like the losses of two of my children—my daughter, Hope, and later my son, Gabriel, who both died due to a rare metabolic disorder.[1] I remember early on in my grief after Hope's death, driving down Hillsboro Road, looking over at the empty seat beside me and tearfully saying out loud to myself, "There is supposed to be a toddler in a car seat over there. She should be here." But there was just an empty space. In those days I was constantly confronted by an empty bedroom at our house, an empty place at the table, an empty place in the family photo, and a huge empty place in my plans for my family and for my life. Over the years since then, the shape and size of that emptiness have changed. But it is still there.

Maybe you can relate. Perhaps you've picked up this book because "empty" is the best way you know how to describe the reality of your life.

Perhaps it is emptiness brought about by loss—the loss of a job, the loss of someone you loved, the loss of a sense of purpose or significance. Or perhaps the emptiness in your life is punctuated not by what once was but by what has never been. You've never been able to establish and maintain the kinds of relationships you've longed for. Maybe there has never been a ring on your finger or a child in your home, or you've never had the title by your name that you hoped for or the level of lifestyle you've dreamed of. The dreams that you have often sought to downplay, for fear that somehow saying them out loud would serve to crush them and thereby crush you, seem to be out of range or the realm of possibility now.

Or perhaps you can't pinpoint exactly why it is you have this sense of emptiness. You realize that in comparison with so many others around you, you have it good. Yet your soul harbors a persistent sense of disappointment and discontent. It sometimes seems as if the lives of nearly everyone around you are full of purpose and meaning, life and love, fun times and future plans, which magnifies the emptiness in your life.

Sometimes your sense of emptiness haunts you as an undefined yet relentless ache. At other times it overwhelms you as an undeniable agony. It is amazing to me how heavy the weight of emptiness can feel, how much room emptiness can take up in our souls, how much pain can be caused by something that isn't even there.

You may have come to see your emptiness as your *greatest problem*, but I hope to convince you that when God sees the emptiness in your life, he sees it as his *greatest opportunity*. In fact, throughout the chapters of this book, we're going to see that emptiness has never been, and never will be, a problem to God. Rather, we're going to see again and again throughout the story the Bible tells us that God does his best work with empty, as by his Spirit he fills it with himself.[2]

God does his best work with empty, as by his Spirit he fills it with himself.

This is good news—but I understand that it may not sound good to you. For some of you, this may sound like a spiritual sales pitch for something that doesn't have the power to make any difference in your day-to-day reality. While there may be some things you want *from* God, perhaps, if you're honest, you're not really interested in getting more *of* God. Perhaps that sounds ethereal, unappealing, or restricting to you. There is something else, someone else you're convinced you must have to fill up the empty place.

Perhaps that's because your view of God and his goodness and what it means to have him at the center of your life has become somehow altered from reality. Perhaps the enemy of your soul, who would love nothing better than to keep you trapped in an echo chamber of emptiness, has convinced you that the suggestion that God could fill your emptiness is a false promise, religious double-talk, or something that, though you might be able to capture it for a moment, simply will not last.

I want you to know at the outset that I have no interest in making false promises or simply filling up some pages with cheer-you-up, convince-you-things-aren't-that-bad, go-out-there-and-enjoy-life, just-take-hold-of-your-destiny motivational mumbo jumbo. I have no five simple steps to getting rid of that nagging emptiness, no self-help formulas for feeling better. And my intention is not to make this book center on my own experiences of emptiness being filled, though I must tell you that I have experienced the incredible joy of being filled up by Christ in ways I could not have imagined.

I want to let God speak for himself. That's what he does in the Bible—all of it. God speaks. He reveals himself. He calls us to himself. He offers to fill us with himself.

I want to draw back the curtain to look with you into the fullness of all that God is and does in regard to the emptiness inherent to life in this world. I want to turn up the volume on his promises so that you might find them both believable and impossible to avoid. And I want to believe with you that God can and will fill up your emptiness in a way that nothing and no one else can.

We might as well begin at the beginning. The very beginning. The beginning of everything—except God.

> In the beginning God created the heavens and
> the earth. The earth was formless and empty,
> and darkness covered the deep waters.
>
> GENESIS 1:1-2

Isn't it interesting that as soon as we learn that God created the earth, we also learn that there were three problems with it? It was formless. It was empty. And it was dark.

But it was not without hope. Why? Because "the Spirit of God was hovering over the surface of the waters" (Genesis 1:2).

The Spirit of God was hovering or fluttering like a dove over the dark and formless emptiness. It was as if something was about to happen. And sure enough, it did.

> Then God said, "Let there be light," and there was light.
> GENESIS 1:3

The problem of darkness was eradicated as creation was flooded with light.

> Then he separated the light from the darkness. God called the light "day" and the darkness "night." . . . Then God said, "Let there be a space between the waters, to separate the waters of the heavens from the waters of the earth." And that is what happened. . . . God called the space "sky."
> GENESIS 1:4-8

Once again, just by God's speaking light and sky into being, the problem of formlessness was dealt with.

God brought order and shape to the environment and the firmament of his creation.

Next he began to deal with the emptiness. We read:

> Then God said, "Let the land sprout with vegetation—every sort of seed-bearing plant, and trees that grow seed-bearing fruit."
>
> GENESIS 1:11

He went on to fill the seas with fish, the skies with birds, and the land with animals. Then he populated the world with human beings made in his own image. God was at work, filling up the emptiness with light and life, beauty and goodness, meaning and relationship.

And this, my friend, is exactly what he wants to do in your life.

As the story of the Bible continues in Genesis, we're introduced to the couple—Abram and Sarai, later called Abraham and Sarah—through whom God intended to fill up the emptiness of the world with descendants as numerous as the stars in the sky and the grains of sand on the shore. Except there was a problem.

> Sarai was unable to become pregnant and had no children.
>
> GENESIS 11:30

It is interesting the way Moses, as the writer of Genesis, seems to emphasize the emptiness of Sarai's womb by expressing the same reality twice: Unable to become pregnant. No children.

But once again, there was hope because God was at work. In fact, he went to work in a way that made it impossible for anyone to miss that he was the one filling the emptiness.

When Sarah overheard God telling Abraham that she was going to give birth to a son, she laughed. It was truly laughable. She was in her nineties and Abraham was one hundred years old. "Is anything too hard for the LORD?" God said (Genesis 18:14). And sure enough, we read, "The LORD kept his word and did for Sarah exactly what he had promised. She became pregnant, and she gave birth to a son for Abraham in his old age. This happened at just the time God had said it would" (Genesis 21:1-2).

What was too hard—in fact, impossible—for Abraham and Sarah to make happen was, in fact, not too hard for God. They named the baby Isaac, which means "laughter." God filled Sarah's empty womb with joy.

Of course, in many ways, it was Sarah's unlikely pregnancy by the power of God that prepared God's people for another unlikely pregnancy years later. What was startling about this pregnancy was not that the woman was old but that she had never been with a man.

> "Don't be afraid, Mary," the angel told her,
> "for you have found favor with God! You will
> conceive and give birth to a son, and you
> will name him Jesus. He will be very great
> and will be called the Son of the Most High.
> The Lord God will give him the throne of his
> ancestor David. And he will reign over Israel
> forever; his Kingdom will never end!"
>
> Mary asked the angel, "But how can this
> happen? I am a virgin."
>
> The angel replied, "The Holy Spirit will
> come upon you, and the power of the Most
> High will overshadow you."
>
> LUKE 1:30-35

Once again the Spirit was hovering, doing his creative work, so that Mary's empty womb was filled with the very life of God. In the darkness of her womb the one who called himself the Light of the World took shape. Cells generated cells. The Word became flesh and he was full—full of grace and truth.

Do you find yourself in need of grace to fill and redeem and relieve the ache of your emptiness? God will fill your life with the grace that only he can provide. And he loves to give grace. John 1:16 tells us, "For from his fullness we have all received, grace upon grace" (ESV).

As you work your way through the pages that follow, my hope and desire is that you will find page after page of grace, page after page of tangible hope that your emptiness can be filled. My prayer is that you'll begin to believe and experience that, in fact, God really does do his best work with empty as he fills it with himself.

CHAPTER ONE

A STRONG CRAVING

God Fills Our Emptiness
with His Provision

IT DIDN'T SEEM like too much to expect. I loved my job as a publicist at a Christian publishing company. I was good at my job. And I was looking forward to going back to it part time after I gave birth to my son, Matt. I was quite sure I was so valuable to the company that certainly they would flex to accommodate my desire to be both an at-home mom and an at-work professional. But when I got the written offer with the new job description, title, and salary, I was devastated. It seemed designed to be too bad to say yes to.

I can't think of too many times in my life when I've actually lain facedown on the floor and sobbed. But I did that day. It felt as if something precious to me—a part of me—was being taken away. I felt devalued, unwanted.

A short time later, floundering in the adjustments of new motherhood, I remember saying to my husband, David, "I want my old life back. I want my old job back. I want my old body back. I want my old relationship with you back."

I believed what I was doing at home with Matt was important. But honestly, it just didn't *feel* important. I remember going into the office to clean out my things and finding a message on my desk that one of the publishing company's bestselling authors had called and was asking me to call him back. Now *that* made me feel important.

I had such a strong craving for something that seemed to hold the key to my happiness—being a valued part of that company, that team. And I couldn't imagine how that hunger was ever going to be satisfied by changing diapers and playing on the floor with an infant. I couldn't imagine how I was going to be happy without that work title after my name, that work paycheck being deposited to my account, and that work significance supporting my sense of self.

That craving dominated my life for quite a while, coloring my view of all of the goodness in my life. And I've had plenty of cravings since then, cravings for things that were out of reach, cravings for things I have been unable to make happen. I imagine you have too. We are creatures of desire. We have wants. And sometimes those wants become cravings—cravings that cause us to lose perspective, cravings so strong that they become the knothole through which we see all of life.

That's how it was for the people of God who were rescued from slavery in Egypt. God rescued them so that they could live with him in his Promised Land, where he pledged to satisfy them with good things. He brought them to the edge of the land he had promised to give them, but they became afraid. They didn't trust him. So they ended up spending forty years in the wilderness. Forty years of in-between time in an inhospitable environment.

But God did not intend for their wilderness years to be wasted years. Rather, he intended to use their time in the wilderness to teach and train them. He intended for them to learn that he could be trusted to provide for his own. Forty years in the wilderness would give them time to live out that belief and depend on him day by day to meet their needs, even if he didn't assuage all of their cravings. There in the wilderness he gave them the opportunity to discover what they really needed more than what they craved.

We read their story of forty years in the wilderness in the books of Exodus, Numbers, and Deuteronomy. But we shouldn't read it merely as a story about distant, disconnected people. What we must see is that their story is our story. If God has rescued you from slavery to sin through the blood of an innocent lamb—the Lamb of God who takes away the sin of the world—and if by faith you have taken hold of God's covenant promises to his people centered in the person of Jesus Christ, then the Israelites' story is your story too.

Just as God did not intend for their years in the wilderness to be wasted, neither does God intend for the years you and I spend living in the empty wilderness of life in this world to be wasted. Just as he wanted to teach and train the Israelites as they made their way through the wilderness, so he has something he wants to teach you and me, a way he wants to train us.

Hunger in the Wilderness

It was one month after the people had left Egypt, and evidently the thrill of escape was beginning to wear off.

> "If only the LORD had killed us back in Egypt," they moaned [to Moses]. "There we sat around pots filled with meat and ate all the bread we wanted. But now you have brought us into this wilderness to starve us all to death."
>
> EXODUS 16:3

Here's the first hint that their craving was robbing them of perspective. They were forgetting about the beatings, the backbreaking work, and the murder of their infant sons back in Egypt. And what was making them forget? Hunger. Their mouths were watering as they remembered the food they ate back in Egypt. But God, in fact, had not brought them into the wilderness to starve. He intended to provide for them.

> Then the LORD said to Moses, "Look, I'm going to rain down food from heaven for you. Each day the people can go out and pick up as much food as they need for that day. I will test them in this to see whether or not they will follow my instructions."
>
> EXODUS 16:4

The Israelites were out in the desert where there was no food or water. And why were they there? Because God had led them there. It wasn't an accidental detour but rather a purposeful detour. He intended to test them. In other words, he was giving them the opportunity to live as if they had a relationship with the God of the universe, who was committed to taking care of them—a relationship expressed on their part by their willingness to trust and obey him.

When the dew evaporated, a flaky substance
as fine as frost blanketed the ground. The
Israelites were puzzled when they saw it. "What
is it?" they asked each other. They had no idea
what it was.

And Moses told them, "It is the food the
LORD has given you to eat."

EXODUS 16:14-15

The Hebrew word *man hu'*, or *manna*, means, "What
is it?" That's what the Israelites called this miraculous
food that was sent to them by God every morning for
forty years. "What's for supper?" someone would ask,
and the answer was always "What is it?" The manna was
a daily miracle that lasted for forty years.

But it was also a daily test. The people could never
store up manna for the next day. Every morning, as they
gathered just enough for that day, they had the opportunity to demonstrate that they trusted God to provide
for them tomorrow too. They had the opportunity to
live by faith.

And really, as we find ourselves living here in the
wilderness of the world, we're put to the same test. In
fact, perhaps that is why God has allowed us to experience the emptiness we feel. Perhaps we're being put to
the test. Or another way to look at it is this:

God is giving us the opportunity to live out what we say we believe.

God intends to use this time in our lives to train us to trust that he will provide what we need, when we need it. Have you said that the God of the Bible is your God? Here in the wilderness is where you have the opportunity to live that out. As you trust him to supply what you really need and refuse to grumble about his provision, you demonstrate that the faith you claim is genuine and not merely a convenient or culturally acceptable alliance.

We catch up with the Israelites in the book of Numbers. It's about a year later, and we discover that even though they had been waking up to manna delivered outside their tents every morning, they were grumbling again.

> *God intends to use this time in our lives to train us to trust that he will provide what we need, when we need it.*

Then the foreign rabble who were traveling with the Israelites began to crave the good things of Egypt. And the people of Israel also began to complain. "Oh, for some meat!" they exclaimed. "We remember the fish we used to eat for free in Egypt. And we had all the

cucumbers, melons, leeks, onions, and garlic we
wanted. But now our appetites are gone. All we
ever see is this manna!"

NUMBERS 11:4-6

Ah, so it's not that they had *nothing* to eat. It's that
they wanted something to eat other than the manna
God rained down on them every day. God was lead-
ing them to a land flowing with milk and honey, and
feeding them day by day with bread from heaven. (And
how do you think bread that is made in heaven tastes?
Heavenly, of course!) But their mouths were watering
for the leeks and melons back in Egypt.

Often people say that if God would do a miracle,
then they would believe in him. Perhaps you think
that if God would simply supply what you are hungry for, then you would be more inclined to trust him
going forward. You would love him rather than resent
him. But the history of Israel is the story of people
who experienced miracles on a massive scale, including the daily miracle of manna waiting for them outside their tents, yet did not trust God. They refused to
love him with all of their hearts, souls, and strength.
Instead of believing in him, they rebelled against
him. As Dr. Tuck Bartholomew says, "They became
one-dimensional people who thought about life only

through the knothole of their craving."[3] Their desire for more variety in their diet became a demand that blinded them to anything and everything else. They couldn't see the goodness of God literally raining down on them because they were consumed by their craving.

Many of us have cravings that blind us so we can't see all that God has done for us and all he has given to us. Yes, we appreciate salvation and all that, but what we *really* crave is to be thin, to have a nicer house in a better neighborhood, to be elevated to a position with more authority and opportunity, to have a child or to be able to change the child we've got.

For the Israelites, everything was about food. What is everything about for you? Are you allowing that craving to be the knothole through which you view all of life, causing you to lose sight of God's goodness?[4]

Consider what the Israelites were craving: the culinary delights of Egypt. They were entertaining the idea of going back to Egypt, the place that had literally been killing them, all because their food cravings could be satisfied there. They were facing a clear choice: Would they follow their cravings back into the slavery of Egypt, or would they be satisfied for now, accepting and enjoying God's provision, believing that he would supply their needs, if not all of their cravings, while they lived in this in-between time in the wilderness? Would they demand that God give them everything they craved in the here and now, or would they allow their hunger to fuel their longing for the day when they would feast with God in the land of milk and honey?

And, of course, we face the same clear choice. God is putting us to the same test.

He is giving us the opportunity to reject what the world offers as we wait for what is to come.

The day is coming when the dissatisfaction that is inherent to life in the wilderness will be gone for good. We'll make our home in God's eternal land, the new heaven and new earth, and we'll never go hungry again. But here and now, as we live out our days in the wilderness of the world, we have the opportunity to wean our appetites away from the things the world provides that temporarily satisfy our taste buds but actually rob us of life and freedom. We have the opportunity to feed on the bread that God provides so that we develop our appetites for what truly nourishes and gives life.

> *As we live out our days in the wilderness of the world, we have the opportunity to wean our appetites away from the things the world provides that temporarily satisfy our taste buds but actually rob us of life and freedom.*

Developing a New Appetite

The Israelites had forty years to develop their appetites for what would really satisfy them. In fact, when the next generation was preparing to enter into the Promised Land, Moses explained to them that this was exactly why God had allowed his people to experience hunger in the wilderness in the first place.

> Remember how the LORD your God led you through the wilderness for these forty years, humbling you and testing you to prove your character, and to find out whether or not you would obey his commands. Yes, he humbled you by letting you go hungry and then feeding you with manna, a food previously unknown to you and your ancestors. He did it to teach you that people do not live by bread alone; rather, we live by every word that comes from the mouth of the LORD.
>
> DEUTERONOMY 8:2-3

Evidently it wasn't an accident that they went some time without food and felt the discomfort of hunger before God sent the manna. What they perceived as lack or emptiness was actually a gift that would help them learn something. By depending upon God's promise to provide manna day by day, the Israelites were to learn that "we live by every word that comes from the mouth of the LORD."

What were the words that come from the mouth of the Lord that they were to live by? God's promise to give them the land; his promised blessings for obedience and curses for disobedience; his assurance that the law was for their good always; his instructions for sacrifice and sanctification, feasts, and festivals; and the announcement of his intention to bless the whole world through them.

As the Word of God begins to change how we think, we discover that it is also changing how we feel. In fact, we discover that it is actually changing what we want.

Of course we have so much more revelation from God than they had. They had the words from God that Moses had delivered to them, but we have the whole of the Bible. So then, what does it mean for you and me to "live by every word that comes from the mouth of the LORD"? It means that we are meant to consume what God has provided to us in his Word by reading it and hearing it preached. We have to chew on it. We have to work its nourishment into our system. We have to think! We find ourselves provided for and strengthened as we think through Scripture's implications and applications and as we figure out what it will look like for us to begin living in light of its truth. And as the Word of God begins to change how we think, we discover that it is also changing how we feel. In fact, we discover that it is actually changing what we want.

For example, we read in the Psalms:

> The Lord God is our sun and our shield.
>   He gives us grace and glory.
> The Lord will withhold no good thing
>   from those who do what is right.
> O Lord of Heaven's Armies,
>   what joy for those who trust in you.
>
> PSALM 84:11-12

Instead of rushing through the passage or discounting it, we begin to meditate on it and tease out its implications. We think about what it means to have Jesus as the one who shines light into our lives so we can see and grow, and what it means to have him as our shield, protecting us, guarding our lives from the enemy of our souls. We begin to think through the many times we've witnessed God give grace to people who don't deserve it—both people in our lives and those we read about in Scripture—and the times in which he has extended grace to us over the course of our lives. We consider the ways in which we can testify that it is really true that the Spirit of Christ has been at work in our lives making us more like Christ, the ways in which he is giving his own glory to us.

Further, as we read and linger on the line, "The Lord will withhold no good thing from those who do what is right," we remember that we read the whole of the Bible through the lens of the life, death, and resurrection of Jesus. We're comforted in knowing that we can expect that the Lord will withhold no good thing from us, not because we have always done what is right but because Jesus has always done what is right, and when we come to him in faith, he transfers his perfect record of obedience to us. Then we think through what the psalmist might mean by "good thing," and we let the reality settle in our souls that God knows what is good better than we do. As we mull the words over in our minds, it becomes clearer to us that since the Lord will withhold no good thing from those who do what is right, whatever he has withheld from us is because it would not be best for us, or because now is not the right time for us to have it. We experience joy trusting in the Lord as our provider.

In other words, rather than feeding on our disappointment and frustration, we choose to chew on nourishing truth. Instead of feeding on social media, where we are bombarded with images of what other people have that has so far been withheld from us, we feed on God's promises of his intentions to do good to us.

So I have to ask you: How's your diet these days? What are you feeding on? Are you allowing your appetite to be developed by the Word of God, or is it mostly shaped by what Egypt has to offer and tells you you must have? God is providing you with an opportunity during these years spent living in the wilderness:

He is giving you the opportunity to discover what you really need, rather than being consumed by what you crave.

Oh, how I wish I would have grasped this in those early days of motherhood when I was so consumed by my craving for significance through my job. How I wish I would have had a heart to learn all that God intended to teach me in those wilderness years that seemed so mundane. He was giving me the opportunity to discover that my significance can never really be dependent on a title or a paycheck. It has to come from him. Jesus alone is the only thing I must have in this world to be happy. As I feed on him, I continue to find that he is what I really need.

If you and I feed only on our own thoughts and feelings, we'll grumble and grow resentful. But as we feed on the Word of God, we'll grow in gratitude for all that

God has provided, and we'll grow in anticipation for all that is yet to be provided.

Another Test of Hunger in the Wilderness

We would like to be able to look back at the family history we read about in Exodus, Numbers, and Deuteronomy and discover that our spiritual ancestors learned what they were meant to learn in the wilderness, that they developed an appetite for God's Word that continued when they moved into the land God provided for them. But they didn't. Instead, when they moved into Canaan, they began to consume all of the idolatry the Canaanites served up to them.

Ultimately, the people of Israel, whom God referred to as his "firstborn son," failed the test of the wilderness. So God sent another Son. And he let this Son experience hunger in the wilderness too.

Then Jesus was led by the Spirit into the wilderness to be tempted there by the devil. For forty days and forty nights he fasted and became very hungry.

During that time the devil came and said to him, "If you are the Son of God, tell these stones to become loaves of bread."

But Jesus told him, "No! The Scriptures say,

'People do not live by bread alone,
   but by every word that comes from the mouth
   of God.'"

MATTHEW 4:1-4

God let Jesus hunger in the wilderness, not for forty years, but for forty days. But instead of grumbling, instead of accusing God of bringing him out into the wilderness to let him die, instead of taking it into his own hands to provide for himself, Jesus trusted in God's provision. Jesus demonstrated that he had spent the previous thirty years of his life feeding on every word that comes from the mouth of God, and it strengthened him for facing hunger in the wilderness with faith that God would provide what he needed.

Hunger on the Hillside

A day came when Jesus found himself in front of a hungry crowd. It was nearly time for the Jewish Passover celebration, the time when the people feasted in celebration of the rescue God had accomplished through Moses centuries before. So Jesus used the timely opportunity to give them a sign about who he is and why he came.

Then Jesus took the loaves, gave thanks to God,
and distributed them to the people. Afterward
he did the same with the fish. And they all ate
as much as they wanted.

JOHN 6:11

As the people experienced the miracle of provision,
they began to think that Jesus was another Moses,
that the miracle that took place in the wilderness for
forty years was beginning again. So the next day, they
got into boats and crossed the Sea of Galilee to get to
Capernaum, hopeful that Jesus would repeat the miracle of the previous day.

"Show us a miraculous sign if you want us to
believe in you. What can you do? After all,
our ancestors ate manna while they journeyed
through the wilderness! The Scriptures say,
'Moses gave them bread from heaven to eat.'"
Jesus said, "I tell you the truth, Moses didn't
give you bread from heaven. My Father did.
And now he offers you the true bread from
heaven. The true bread of God is the one who
comes down from heaven and gives life to the
world."
"Sir," they said, "give us that bread every day."

Jesus replied, "I am the bread of life. Whoever comes to me will never be hungry again."

JOHN 6:30-35

The people were correct to relate the miracle that happened in their day to the story of what happened in Moses' day. But they were missing the point of the miracle. They were missing what the sign was pointing to. Jesus isn't merely the conduit of God's promise of bread, as Moses was. Jesus *is* the bread. And Jesus was standing there offering himself to them.

Now what would have made sense at this point was for them to come to him—in fact, run to him. But instead, they did something that sounds very familiar to us, having just read the story of their ancestors—our ancestors—in the wilderness. They grumbled.

[Jesus said,] "I am the living bread that came down from heaven. Anyone who eats this bread will live forever; and this bread, which I will offer so the world may live, is my flesh."

Then the people began arguing with each other about what he meant. "How can this man give us his flesh to eat?" they asked.

So Jesus said again, "I tell you the truth, unless you eat the flesh of the Son of Man and drink his blood, you cannot have eternal life within you. But anyone who eats my flesh and drinks my blood has eternal life, and I will raise that person at the last day."

JOHN 6:51-54

At this point, many of those who had been following Jesus turned away and deserted him. They only wanted bread from Jesus, not Jesus as bread. They were thinking that Jesus would be useful in their pursuit of the life they wanted, but they didn't really want *him*. They just wanted what they thought he could give to them.

And when we read this, we can't help but see ourselves in these people. We think life—the good life—will come when Jesus gives us what we want, what we think we need. And just as he did with these people in Capernaum, he presses the issue with us to the point of offense. Jesus stands offering himself to us, and he's asking, "Will you feed on my atoning death as your life? Will you abide in me, feed on me, commune with me? Will you love me? Will you nurture your craving for me rather than insisting on having what you crave?"

Perhaps we're not as immediately dismissive of Jesus' offer of himself as the people were that day in

Capernaum. We may be more polite, yet our attitudes and actions often say, "Jesus, thank you. I respect you and appreciate the offer. But if you really want to be helpful, you would add to my bank account, or add to my family, or add to the estimation others have of me." And Jesus looks us in the eyes and says, "Don't you understand? If you don't feed on me, you will starve to death. But as you feed on me, you take my own unlimited, unstoppable, unending life into yourself."

What a tragedy it would be for Jesus to supply everything on our wish lists yet leave our deepest need unmet, for him to shower us with what we want yet leave us empty of what we really need.

How Will You Feed Your Hunger?

My friend, I wish I could tell you that God is going to rain down whatever it is that you are so hungry for. I wish I could tell you that he is going to miraculously provide so that you will be filled. There are others who will say that. They'll tell you that if you have enough faith and pray the right prayer and speak the right words, then you will get your miracle. But we see all over Scripture that that just isn't true. I cannot tell you that your need is going to be met in the way and timing you are hoping and praying it will be met. No one can.

But what I can tell you is this: If you are hungry, God

is letting you hunger for a good purpose. God is giving you the opportunity to live out what you say you believe. God is strengthening you by forcing you to reckon with the inability of the things of this world to fill you up and their tendency, instead, to enslave you. God is seeking to retrain your appetite toward what you really need, what will truly satisfy and sustain you, what will infuse your life with lasting significance. God is whispering to you, or perhaps shouting to you in your emptiness, "Taste and see that the LORD is good" (Psalm 34:8).

Are you open to that? Or does that just sound like an empty religious answer that will leave you continuing to crave?

I can think of times when I have felt as if someone were giving me the pat answer, the spiritualized answer that I was certain I saw right through. I was quite sure that I was hearing just another worn-out version of "Get close to God by reading your Bible and praying" that simply would not work. At least I didn't think it would work for me. And maybe you think that what I'm saying to you right now is just a pat answer that you've heard before and that is really no answer at all. Perhaps you think there is no way that something as spiritual-sounding as feeding on Christ day by day, hour by hour, would have any power to address your deep need.

But perhaps that's because you've never really tried

it. Perhaps you've dabbled in it but never truly feasted on him. I wish I could look you in the eyes when I tell you that it is true that as we begin to chew on "every word that comes from the mouth of God"—not just by checking off a daily Bible reading, but by tearing off huge chunks of Scripture to think about, figure out, pray through, and submit to—we find that our cravings don't have as much power over us as they once did. As we make time day by day to simply savor who Jesus is and all he has done, is doing, and will do for us, rather than rushing through a fast-food meal of Netflix, Internet scrolling, and other diversions, we find ourselves tasting and seeing that the Lord is good. It's not that we're not hungry anymore; it's that our appetites are changing. We are discovering that Jesus is not someone we use to get a feast that's to our liking. Rather, Jesus is the feast.

As you feed on his obedient life, you'll lose your appetite for perfection and performance. As you feed on his sacrificial death, you'll be able to enjoy drawing close to God rather than living in fear of being under the judgment of God. And as you feed on his victorious resurrection, anchoring your hopes in the resurrection body that will be given to you, the heavenly inheritance that will be granted to you, and the eternal life that will be extended to you one day, you'll find that you stop expecting that this world could ever fill you up with its limited offerings. Every time you participate in eating the bread and drinking the cup of the Lord's Supper, rather than rushing through it mindlessly, you'll savor the taste on your tongue, allowing it to fill you with anticipation of the greater feast to come, when the Lord "will spread a wonderful feast for all the people of the world. It will be a delicious banquet with clear, well-aged wine and choice meat" (Isaiah 25:6).

I want and need my appetites to be retrained toward that feast more and more each day. Don't you?

You and I live in a day when high-protein or high-fat diets have made bread the enemy of our weight-management goals. So perhaps when we hear Jesus offer himself as the Bread of Life, we think we'll stick with the low-carb option. But for the Israelites in the wilderness, and for the people in Capernaum, to not have bread to eat was to starve. To say no to bread was not merely to live a diminished life; it was to have no life. The options were to eat this bread or starve to death.

And really, my friend, it is the same for us. We feed on this bread, the person and work of Jesus Christ, or we starve in the wilderness of this world. You see, it is not just that nothing else will fill up our emptiness; it's that nothing else will nourish our souls. Nothing else can provide the life we are so hungry for.

CHAPTER TWO

A TENT AT
THE CENTER

God Fills Our Emptiness

with His Presence

SOMETIMES I FEEL LONELY.

There, I said it. Honestly, it's a little embarrassing to admit. It takes me back to the uncomfortable feelings I had in junior high and high school (okay—college, too) when I didn't have anyone to sit with in the cafeteria.

If I look at my life objectively, I really don't have any reason to feel lonely. I have a good marriage to a fine man who loves me well; I have an adult son who makes me smile every time he walks in my door; I interact with the most amazing and interesting people through my work; I have close friends with whom I share delicious meals and happy times; I have a church home filled with brothers and sisters who care about me and pray for me.

And yet . . . there are times when I feel really lonely.

Of course, there's a big difference between feeling lonely and being alone. I can be alone and not feel lonely at all. Conversely, some of my loneliest experiences have been when I was in a crowd of people.

Evidently I am not alone when it comes to loneliness. Former surgeon general Dr. Vivek Murthy recently described loneliness as "an epidemic."[5] Similarly, in 2018, former prime minister of Britain Theresa May appointed a "minister for loneliness" to tackle the social and health issues caused by social isolation.[6]

Perhaps loneliness is meant to serve as an invitation into something we should actually pursue at great cost—intimate fellowship with the God who made us and is with us.

But I'm not sure loneliness is a problem that can be solved by better health care or social systems. In fact, I'm not sure that loneliness is really a problem to be solved. Perhaps it isn't something to be avoided at all costs. Instead, perhaps loneliness is meant to serve as an invitation into something we should actually pursue at great cost—intimate fellowship with the God who made us and is with us.

We might like to think we are spiritual enough to engage with God on our own, without anything or anyone urging us in that direction. But if that's what we think, we're just fooling ourselves.

> No one is truly wise;
>> no one is seeking God.
> All have turned away.
>
> ROMANS 3:11-12, QUOTING PSALM 14:2-3

If, as Paul says, "no one is seeking God" on their own, what might cause us to have any interest in or desire for him? We'd have to need him. We'd have to need what only he can provide.

Of course, we sometimes think that connection with people is what we need most, that if we can just find the right people and build the right kind of community, all of our needs for companionship will be met. Somehow we see connection with God as something wholly separate from connection with others, as something relegated to the religious realm, or perhaps even as something optional for when we're in the mood or in a crisis.

But we are kidding ourselves if we think that the finite human beings who come in and out of our personal worlds can meet all of our needs for connection. No matter how close people come, no matter how kind and consistent they are, it won't be enough. We will always have a need to be intimately connected to our creator, the lover of our souls, the only one who will ever know us completely and love us perfectly and unendingly. And perhaps it is only a sense of loneliness that gets us thinking and moving in his direction.

Augustine wrote about God, "You have made us for yourself, and our hearts are restless till they find their rest in Thee."[7] When Augustine says that God made us "for" himself, we could also translate his meaning as "toward" himself. Peter Kreeft writes, "We exist 'to' or 'toward' or 'in movement to' Him, like arrows moving toward a target or homing pigeons flying home."[8]

If this is true, then loneliness is the whisper of God himself, wooing us and calling us home to himself.

But all of this raises a question—at least in my mind: Why would God want to be in relationship with us mere mortals? You see, the Bible reveals something about God that honestly, I sometimes find very difficult to believe: *He wants to be with us.*

He chooses us, pursues us, redeems us, and sanctifies us because . . . he wants to be *with* us. We often think that God's work in our lives is about what we will be able to *achieve for* him, but that is a misunderstanding of his heart and his purpose. His work in our lives is a reflection of his desire for us to *be with* him.

He doesn't woo us to himself to meet his own need.

He has no needs.[9] God is complete in himself; he is not lonely. God . . . is . . . love. The persons of the triune God—Father, Son, and Holy Spirit—have eternally existed in perfect communion with each other, and it is this communion we are invited into. The Father chooses us and the Spirit joins us to the Son so that we can be welcomed into this divine love that has eternally preceded us, is infinitely above us, yet is genuinely for us.

How do we know that this love God has for us works its way out in his desire to be with us? It is woven into the story of the Bible from beginning to end. And the more we understand and find ourselves in this story, the more power it has to lead us into experiencing the presence of God in our lives in a way that soothes the ache of loneliness.

God Came Down to Be with Us in a Garden

The Bible begins by telling us about the home, or sanctuary, that God created to share with those made in his own image—the Garden of Eden. Adam and Eve were there enjoying God's personal presence with them . . . until sin sent them into hiding from God. Genesis 3 is the first time we read in the Bible about God coming down to be among his people. And we discover in it something important about God's presence:

When God comes down, he comes down in the completeness of who he is. God is completely loving. But he is also completely holy and completely just. Up to this point his holiness had presented no problem to Adam and Eve, but now they had sinned against that holiness. And as much as God longs to be with his people, he cannot tolerate sin and its corruption in his presence. So when the story of the Bible had only just begun, it took a detour—one that moved humanity further away from the presence of God.

The story of the Bible could have ended right there with God coming down in judgment. Except that even as he came down in judgment, he also came down in mercy, covering Adam and Eve with animal skins to hide their shame. God made a promise to the serpent who had tempted them—that one day a descendant of Adam and Eve would crush his head, halting his evil and bringing an end to the separation and alienation between God and his people (see Genesis 3:15).

When God comes down, he comes down in the completeness of who he is.

Even though Adam and Eve were ejected from the presence of God in the Garden of Eden, God's intention to be with his people did not change. Instead,

God began working out his plan to bring his people back into his presence. He began by calling one man to leave everything and everyone he had ever known and to go to a new country where he knew no one. And, amazingly, he went. It was there that God took a tangible, visible step toward his people. We read that "the LORD appeared to Abram. . . . And Abram built an altar there" (Genesis 12:7). God made incredible promises to Abraham—promises that included not only what God would do for him (make him great, give him descendants and land) and how God would use him (to bless every family of the earth through him) but also who God intended to be to him. The Lord told him, "This is the everlasting covenant: I will always be your God and the God of your descendants after you" (Genesis 17:7).

Do you hear the intimacy in what God said to Abraham? He did not merely say, "I will be God" but rather "I will always be *your* God." This is personal. Over the course of generations, God kept repeating the promise of his personal presence to Abraham's descendants, saying, "I will be with you" (see Genesis 26:3; Exodus 3:12; Joshua 1:5; Judges 6:16; 1 Kings 11:38; and Isaiah 43:2).

There were seventy-two descendants in Abraham's family when they went to Egypt in search of bread during a famine. When Moses finally led the Israelites out of Egypt four hundred years later, they were a nation of more than two million people. God came down on Mount Sinai, where he wrote on stone tablets how his people were to live once they entered into the land that he was giving to them. They weren't going alone; he intended to live there with them, among them. He told them, "I will walk among you; I will be your God, and you will be my people" (Leviticus 26:12).

God Came Down to Be with Us in a Tent

There at the mountain, God also gave Moses blueprints for a tent. His people were out there in the wilderness living in tents, and he wanted to be with them. So he had them build him a tent—a very special one, built to particular specifications, called the Tabernacle.

When we read through the book of Exodus, it's a little surprising just how many chapters are given over to describing the design and construction of this tent in great detail (see Exodus 25–31). Reading the story, you get a sense that this tent is very important to God. Why? Because being with his people is important to him. God wanted to live in a tent in the center of the camp because he wanted to be at the center of his people's lives.

Once the construction of the Tabernacle was complete and the furniture and curtains were in place, we read,

Then the cloud covered the Tabernacle, and the glory of the LORD filled the Tabernacle. Moses could no longer enter the Tabernacle because the cloud had settled down over it, and the glory of the LORD filled the Tabernacle. . . . The cloud of the LORD hovered over the Tabernacle during the day, and at night fire glowed inside the cloud so the whole family of Israel could see it. This continued throughout all their journeys.

EXODUS 40:34-35, 38

The people could see the fiery presence of God right there in the camp at night, hovering over the Tabernacle as a cloud as God himself dwelt in the Most Holy Place. Whenever the cloud moved, the whole camp moved. And after forty years in the wilderness, they moved into the land of Canaan, where God intended to live among them permanently as their God.

There, generations later, Solomon built a more permanent dwelling place for God, the Temple in Jerusalem. It had the same basic design as the Tabernacle and was made with the finest materials by the finest craftsmen. And once again, when the Temple was completed and the Ark of the Covenant was brought into its inner sanctuary,

A thick cloud filled the Temple of the
LORD. The priests could not continue their
service because of the cloud, for the glorious
presence of the LORD filled the Temple of the
LORD. Then Solomon prayed, "O LORD, you
have said that you would live in a thick cloud
of darkness. Now I have built a glorious Temple
for you, a place where you can live forever!"

1 KINGS 8:10-13

Solomon celebrated the presence of God among
his people in the Most Holy Place of the Temple and
prayed that God would live there forever. How amazing
to have the visible presence of the one true God right
there in their beautiful Temple at the center of their
capital city!

Yet surely this was not all that God intended his
presence among his people to be. Yes, he was there
among them, but ordinary Israelites had no access to
him. Only the appointed priests could come into the
Holy Place of the Temple. Only one person—the high
priest—could enter into the Most Holy Place where
God dwelled. And he could come in only once a year.

There was still so much distance, such a significant barrier between God and his people. Surely God
wanted to live among his people in a more accessible

way than that—in a way that his people could see him and come close to him.

Yes, he did. Yes, he does.

God Came Down to Be with Us in the Flesh

The day came when, as the apostle John put it, "the Word became human and made his home among us" (John 1:14). Or, as Paul put it:

> Though he was God,
>> he did not think of equality with God
>> as something to cling to.
> Instead, he gave up his divine privileges;
>> he took the humble position of a slave
>> and was born as a human being.
>
> PHILIPPIANS 2:6-7

God came down, not in the form of cloud or fire but in human flesh. His coming into the world as one of us was yet another step in working out his plan to be with his people.

You see, if we, as sinners, were ever going to be able to live in God's presence, our sin had to be dealt with. We like to think about the perfect love of God. But God is not only perfectly loving. He is also perfectly just and perfectly holy. His perfect justice requires that our sin be punished. His perfect holiness requires that our sin be purged. And that's why Jesus came. That's why when Jesus breathed his last breath on the cross, the curtain in the sanctuary of the Temple was torn in two, from top to bottom. He absorbed the punishment for our sin so it is no longer a barrier between us and God.

On the cross, Jesus not only absorbed the punishment we deserve; he also experienced the abandonment we deserve. In our loneliest moments, we can find fellowship and companionship with Jesus because he experienced loneliness too. On the cross, Jesus cried out, "My God, my God, why have you forsaken me?" (Matthew 27:46; Mark 15:34, ESV). Jesus experienced the torment of loneliness so that you and I would never be abandoned, never forsaken, never truly alone.

After the death and resurrection of Jesus, not only was there no further need for the curtain in the Temple, there was no further need for the Temple. God no longer intended to descend to dwell on the earth and be confined in a fifteen-foot-by-fifteen-foot room in a building made of stone. God intended to dwell not merely *among* his people but *in* his people.

God Came Down to Be in Us by His Spirit
Forty days after his resurrection, Jesus ascended into heaven, and for a time it seemed to all those who loved

him that he was gone for good. He had told them to stay in Jerusalem until the Father sent them the gift he had promised. And then:

> On the day of Pentecost all the believers were meeting together in one place. Suddenly, there was a sound from heaven like the roaring of a mighty windstorm, and it filled the house where they were sitting. Then, what looked like flames or tongues of fire appeared and settled on each of them. And everyone present was filled with the Holy Spirit and began speaking in other languages, as the Holy Spirit gave them this ability.
>
> ACTS 2:1-4

Just as generations before them had seen the fiery presence of God descend to dwell in the Tabernacle and later the Temple,[10] on this day those who were gathered saw the fiery presence of God descend to dwell in *them*. Never before had ordinary believers experienced the presence of God in this way. Surely in that moment the disciples remembered what Jesus had said to them in the upper room the night before he was crucified:

I will ask the Father, and he will give you
another Advocate, who will never leave you.
He is the Holy Spirit, who leads into all truth.
The world cannot receive him, because it isn't
looking for him and doesn't recognize him. But
you know him, because he lives with you now
and later will be in you.

JOHN 14:16-17

You and I weren't there on that particular day in redemptive history when the Spirit of God became visible by coming down to live inside those who put their faith in Christ. But the Spirit's presence in our lives is no less real. If you have become joined to Christ by faith, it is only because the Spirit has done a work in you to make you spiritually alive (which is called regeneration). The way he did that was to bind you, tether you, join you to Christ.

We tend to talk about becoming a Christian in terms of a decision we've made or a ritual we've experienced. But the Bible speaks of the reality that saves us and secures us and sustains us primarily in terms of being united to Christ. Jesus calls us to repent and believe (see Mark 1:15), and when we do, in a way that gloriously transcends our finite understanding, through repentance and faith, we become joined—*spiritually and bodily*—to the crucified, resurrected, alive-forevermore person of Jesus Christ. The Holy Spirit binds us to Christ and seals us in Christ, so that we can never become separated.

Just think of the vivid imagery the Bible uses to help us grasp this connectedness. Jesus is the Vine and we are the branches (see John 15:5); Jesus is the head and we are his body (see 1 Corinthians 6:15-19); Christ is the foundation and we are living stones joined to the foundation (see 1 Peter 2:4-5); Christ is the bridegroom and we are the bride joined to him in an eternal marriage (see Ephesians 5:25-31).

The Holy Spirit unites us to Christ and creates in us a hunger for communion with Christ. This means that the loneliness you feel might actually be the work of the Holy Spirit in your life, nudging you toward pursuit of greater intimacy with the lover of your soul.

> *For many, or perhaps most of us, communion with Christ comes when we reach the end of ourselves. That's when we're poised for a breakthrough.*

Our lonely times prepare us to enjoy intimate fellowship with Christ.

For many, or perhaps most of us, communion with Christ comes when we reach the end of ourselves. That's when we're poised for a breakthrough. Sometimes we experience this growth through a heightened aware-ness of God at work in our circumstances, awakening our affections and energizing our obedience. Other times it is more ordinary, though no less supernatu-ral, as we experience an ongoing awareness of his near-ness through the daily disciplines of prayer and Bible study.

We find communion with him, and an easing of our loneliness, as we talk to the one who knows us better than anyone else. He has always been and will always be present in our lives. We can tell him any-thing and everything. And, amazingly, he wants to hear anything and everything. He's constantly calling us into the secret place of intimacy with him through prayer. There we can move beyond praying by rote into deeper conversation. We learn to practice his presence as we develop the habit of inviting him into our first thoughts as we awaken in the morning. Even before we get out of bed, we greet him, smiling at the thought of spending another day with him in our lives. Throughout the day, as we carry out ordinary tasks, we continue the conversation, consulting him as we make decisions, thanking him for his kindnesses, ask-ing him to meet our needs. And rather than making our last conversation of the day with someone on a television or smartphone screen, we drift off to sleep conscious that while we rest, he will be present with us, safeguarding us through the night.

This is what it means to experience and practice the presence of God.

As we practice his presence in these ways, we *genuinely* experience his presence. But we don't yet experience it perfectly or completely. That perfect and complete communion is reserved for later.

God Will Come Down Again
to Be with Us Face-to-Face

The day is coming when God's desire to be with us, which progressively develops throughout the story of the Bible, will become the reality that we will live in forever. The apostle John was given a vision of the day. He writes,

> I heard a loud voice from the throne saying,
> "Behold, the dwelling place of God is with man.
> He will dwell with them, and they will be his
> people, and God himself will be with them as
> their God. He will wipe away every tear from
> their eyes, and death shall be no more, neither
> shall there be mourning, nor crying, nor pain
> anymore, for the former things have passed away."
> REVELATION 21:3-4, ESV

53

Notice the personal nature of God's presence—he reaches out his hand to wipe away our tears. He'll be as close to us and as real to us as any person has ever been. John writes that we will "see his face, and his name will be written on [our] foreheads" (Revelation 22:4). Face-to-face conversation, eye-to-eye connection, permanent identification, never-ending communion.

He will be at the center—the center of the heavenly city, the center of our attention, the center of our affections.

No more lonely nights. No more lonely days. No more loneliness at all.

Until then, we have his Spirit dwelling in us, we have an audience with him in prayer, and we have his Word, through which he speaks to us, teaches us, trains us, comforts us, calls us. His Word equips us for the loneliness inherent in this life.

On those days and nights when feelings of loneliness overwhelm us and threaten to define us, God has given us a song to sing to remind us of his presence with us. We can sit outside under the stars or stand where we can take in the expanse of the world God has created and sing or say these words with the psalmist, savoring every image so that it makes an impression on our souls:

I can never escape from your Spirit!
　　I can never get away from your presence!
If I go up to heaven, you are there;
　　if I go down to the grave, you are there.
If I ride the wings of the morning,
　　if I dwell by the farthest oceans,
even there your hand will guide me,
　　and your strength will support me.
I could ask the darkness to hide me
　　and the light around me to become night—
　　but even in darkness I cannot hide from you.
To you the night shines as bright as day.
　　Darkness and light are the same to you. . . .
How precious are your thoughts about me,
　　　　O God.
　　They cannot be numbered!
I can't even count them;
　　they outnumber the grains of sand!
And when I wake up,
　　you are still with me!
PSALM 139:7-12, 17-18

In the emptiness of loneliness, God is reminding us
that we were made for more than any connection we
can find in this world. He is wooing us to himself.

CHAPTER THREE

A DESPERATE NEED

God Fills Our Emptiness with His Grace

I HEARD A PREACHER say one time that we all have dark thoughts about God. My initial response was skepticism. I was highly resistant to the very idea. As someone whose earliest memories are filled with Bible truths, I didn't want to think that I have anything but esteem and love for God.

But I've come to see that the preacher was right. We don't instinctually expect the best of God. We're a bit suspicious of him. We suspect he's out to make us miserable instead of deeply and eternally happy. When the worst happens in our lives, we sometimes respond with a sense of "I knew it . . . I've been waiting for this." We so easily entertain the idea that God is cruelly against us rather than lovingly for us.

The Bible tells the story of a woman who not only entertained the idea that God was against her, she became convinced of it. It's surprising that the little book that contains her story isn't named after her, because it begins with her crisis and ends with the resolution of her crisis.

The book of Ruth begins not with Ruth, but with Naomi, telling us about the time and place in which she lived. The first line of the book explains that she was living in the town of Bethlehem in the days when the judges ruled. In other words, these were the days when there was no king over the loose federation of twelve tribes of Israel that were living in Canaan. The last line of the previous book in the Bible tells us, "In those days Israel had no king; all the people did whatever seemed right in their own eyes" (Judges 21:25). People were doing whatever they pleased, making it a dark and dangerous time to live in Israel.

During this era there was a repeated cycle of God's people doing despicable things, followed by God sending famine or an invader to discipline them, followed by the people crying out to God for relief and salvation. And when the book of Ruth opens, evidently the people of Bethlehem in Judah were experiencing one of those disciplining seasons. They were in the midst of a famine.

Famine in the Land

Let's think for a minute about what that would be like. I have never experienced anything close to a famine. My challenge has always been trying to figure out how to eat less of the abundant food options that surround me, so I can barely imagine what it is like to go to bed hungry every night and wake up hungry every morning, finding no relief.

It was this kind of hunger, a desperate need, that drove one family living in Bethlehem to make a choice that may not immediately seem shocking. Actually, it seems very reasonable to us: They moved.

> A man from Bethlehem in Judah left his home and went to live in the country of Moab, taking his wife and two sons with him. The man's name was Elimelech, and his wife was Naomi. Their two sons were Mahlon and Kilion. They were Ephrathites from Bethlehem in the land of Judah. And when they reached Moab, they settled there.
>
> RUTH 1:1-2

They left the land of famine and moved to a place where they thought they would be able to find something to eat.

Moving is no big deal in our day. But this was a unique time and place and people. The land Naomi and her family were leaving was the Promised Land—the land God gave to his people, the land where he promised to be with them and bless them. Elimelech and his wife and two sons left this land to move, not just anywhere, but to Moab, a country founded centuries earlier through the incestuous relationship of Lot with his daughters, a land in which they worshiped other gods (see Judges 10:6), a land that had oppressed and enslaved the Israelites for eighteen years only a short time before (see Judges 3:14).

This choice would have shocked those around them. Their fellow Israelites would have wanted to say to them, "Don't do it! Don't go! Cry out to God in repentance! Cry out to God to send relief and rain! Put your trust in God to save you and supply you with what you need. Don't seek out some solution apart from God, away from where he has promised to bless his people."

But not only did Naomi's family leave God's land, they settled in far away from it. The boys married Moabite women. But what seemed like a reasonable step for self-preservation proved to provide no lasting preservation at all. Soon the family's story was engraved on grave markers in Moab. First Elimelech died, leaving Naomi a widow in a foreign land. Then both of her sons, Mahlon and Kilion, died. Naomi had gone with her family to Moab in search of life, but she found herself far away from God and far away from God's people with no protection, no source of provision, and seemingly no future.

Grace Comes Down to Bethlehem

Then, into this terribly sad situation came a glimmer of hope. Word reached Naomi that "the LORD had blessed his people in Judah by giving them good crops again" (Ruth 1:6). Grace had come down on the fields of Bethlehem in the form of rain and a growing barley crop, and Naomi wanted in on this grace. So she packed her bags and set out for home, along with her two daughters-in-law. A word starts repeating itself at this point in the narrative of the story—*return*. Naomi was returning to the place and to the people God had promised to bless. A turning or returning always seems to be how the best things begin for people in God's story, and this is no exception.

Along the way, Naomi stopped to encourage her daughters-in-law to go back to their families in Moab. She knew that these Moabite women could not expect a warm welcome in Israel. They would be seen as enemies and outsiders, and their chances of marriage would be slim. But if they went back to Moab, they would likely find husbands and have children and homes. Besides, because Naomi was convinced that God was against her, she told Ruth and Orpah that they couldn't expect anything good if they went with her. "Things are far more bitter for me than for you, because the LORD himself has raised his fist against me," she said (Ruth 1:13).

"Oh, Naomi," we want to say when we've read ahead to see where this story is headed, "God has not raised his fist against you. God's hand is at work in your life. He's drawing you back to the place where he intends to bless you beyond what you can imagine. He's given you a daughter-in-law who will be the conduit of that blessing. You just can't see it at this point in your story."

While one of the daughters-in-law, Orpah, took Naomi's advice and determined to head back to Moab, the other, Ruth, could not be swayed. She had heard about Israel's God and the promises he made to bless his people, and so she bound herself to her bitter mother-in-law and to her mother-in-law's God. God was at work to provide for Naomi through this noble daughter-in-law—but Naomi couldn't see it. Naomi's old friends couldn't see it either. When the two women arrived in

Bethlehem, Naomi's old friends could hardly recognize her, and they said nothing at all about her Moabite companion. It's as if Ruth was invisible to them.

"Don't call me Naomi," she said to the women of the town. To be called "Naomi," which means "pleasant," was a cruel joke to her. "Instead, call me Mara, for the Almighty has made life very bitter for me. I went away full, but the LORD has brought me home empty. Why call me Naomi when the LORD has caused me to suffer and the Almighty has sent such tragedy upon me?" (Ruth 1:20-21).

Clearly Naomi believed in God's sovereignty and in his justice. She saw the events of her life as something God had brought about, but she had no expectation of God's grace or kindness in the midst of the suffering. The presence of tragedy in her life was proof to Naomi that God was against her, and she had settled into having very dark thoughts about God. Perhaps she pictured him standing up in court to testify against her. She could practically hear him saying, "This woman left my land, she turned her back on my promises, and she doesn't deserve anything good. What she deserves is to suffer."

Naomi's understanding of the world, her grasp of God's ways with his people, was that God gives us what we deserve, what we've earned through our good or bad behavior. It was the same understanding Job's friends seemed to have—that in Job's suffering he was getting what he deserved. Naomi and the friends of Job seem to have based their understanding and expectations of God on the law of Moses, which promised blessings for obedience and curses for disobedience. But actually, what we see again and again, from the beginning to the end of the Bible, is that God repeatedly gives his people what they don't deserve. It's called grace. We think we want this life to be fair, but that's not really what we want. In a perfectly fair world, there's no room for grace, for getting what we don't deserve. It is this undeserved favor, the grace of God, that proves to be the defining element in our lives.

In a perfectly fair world, there's no room for grace, for getting what we don't deserve. And it is this undeserved favor, the grace of God, that proves to be the defining element in our lives.

Grace Extended to an Outsider

Naomi was clearly not expecting to experience grace. But amazingly, Ruth was. There in Bethlehem, perhaps at the doorway of the old mud hut Elimelech and Naomi had left behind so many years ago, Ruth told Naomi that she was heading out to glean in the fields of grain "after him in whose sight I shall find favor" (Ruth 2:2, ESV). Ruth headed out the door expecting to find "favor," or grace, in the fields of Bethlehem. She knew about the provisions in God's law for the foreigner and sojourner in Israel, that they were welcome to pick up grain on the edges of the field left behind by the harvesters (see Leviticus 19:9-10), and so she headed out to collect what she could.

The writer of the book of Ruth is having a bit of fun with us as readers when he tells us, "And *as it happened*, she found herself working in a field that belonged to Boaz, the relative of her father-in-law, Elimelech" (Ruth 2:3, emphasis added). Of course this hadn't just happened. God's hand was at work, guiding Ruth to this particular field that was owned by a godly man who stood out among most men in his day, this period when "all the people did whatever seemed right in their own eyes" (Judges 21:25). Boaz was concerned about what was right in God's eyes, and we're going to see that he wanted to do right by the foreigner in his field.

Boaz arrived at his land and asked about the woman he didn't recognize who was gathering grain on the edges of his fields. When his workers told him it was Ruth, the one who had returned to Bethlehem with Naomi, he realized he had heard about her and her commitment to her mother-in-law. Those who worked for him callously referred to Ruth as "the Moabitess," but Boaz called her "my daughter." He seemed to be taking responsibility for her. We sense immediately that he intended to be kind to her.

Boaz said to Ruth, "Listen, my daughter. Stay right here with us when you gather grain; don't go to any other fields. Stay right behind the young women working in my field. See which part of the field they are harvesting, and then follow them. I have warned the young men not to treat you roughly. And when you are thirsty, help yourself to the water they have drawn from the well" (Ruth 2:8-9). He was providing her with both protection and refreshment.

Boaz even prayed a blessing on Ruth, saying, "May the LORD, the God of Israel, under whose wings you have come to take refuge, reward you fully for what you have done" (Ruth 2:12). Boaz was asking God to fill up the life of this young woman with his goodness, his reward, his provision, his protection. This was even more favor than Ruth went to the fields expecting that day. And what Boaz didn't yet know was that he was going to be the answer to his own prayer.

"At mealtime Boaz called to her, 'Come over here, and help yourself to some food. You can dip your bread in the sour wine.' So she sat with his harvesters, and Boaz gave her some roasted grain to eat. She ate all she wanted and still had some left over" (Ruth 2:14). He was being generous to her.

When we read that Ruth ate until she was full and still had some left over, there's something that sounds a bit familiar to us. Where else have we read about people eating their fill and still having baskets of food left over?

Ah, yes. That story from John that we read about in chapter 1 when a crowd of five thousand hungry people was invited to sit down for lunch with Jesus. Jesus took five barley loaves and two fish and distributed them to the people, and when he was done, there were twelve baskets of food left over. Clearly Boaz was showing us something in shadow form about another man of Bethlehem who would be born one day—a greater Boaz, who would fill not only the empty stomachs of multitudes of people but also their empty hearts. He would set before the people a meal of bread and wine that would be a sign to them of the way he intended to nourish and sustain them into eternity.

When Ruth headed back to the mud hut that night, her mother-in-law could hardly believe the huge stash of barley she brought home. It was enough for them to feast on for weeks. And when Ruth told Naomi that she had spent the day gleaning in the fields of Boaz, the name rang a bell for Naomi. "'May the LORD bless him!' Naomi told her daughter-in-law. 'He is showing his kindness to us as well as to your dead husband. That man is one of our closest relatives, one of our family redeemers'" (Ruth 2:20).

Grace Goes to Work in Naomi

Something seems to have been shaking loose the bitterness toward God that had gripped Naomi's heart. Perhaps he was not set against her as she'd thought. The turning that began when she relocated herself physically back to Bethlehem now seemed to be happening spiritually as well. She was asking the Lord to bless this man. She saw God's sovereign guidance of Ruth to this particular field as being a kindness from God to her as well as to her dead husband.

It is easy for us to understand how this could be a kindness to the living—to Naomi and Ruth—as Boaz could save them from starvation and provide a home for them. But how would God's guidance be a kindness to Ruth's dead husband? Clearly there is something below the surface here that may not be obvious to us as modern readers. We get a hint from the rest of Naomi's statement when she said that Boaz was "one of our family redeemers."

Naomi meant that because Boaz was a close relative, he might be able to fulfill the role of family redeemer as provided for in the law God gave to Moses. A redeemer acted as protector, defender, avenger, or rescuer for other members of the family, especially when they experienced loss or injustice. When someone fell into poverty and had to sell his land, his family redeemer could buy it back and restore it to him so that the land allotted to the family in the days of Joshua stayed within the family. And when someone died without an heir, the family redeemer could marry the widow with the aim of producing an heir for the dead husband.

Now we're beginning to understand why Naomi saw that God's guiding Ruth to Boaz could be a kindness to her dead husband. If Boaz were willing to serve as their family redeemer by marrying Ruth, there was a possibility that this union would provide an heir to inherit the land that once belonged to Elimelech. To have property in the Promised Land was to have a stake in the promises of God to his people. And to die without an heir meant that a family's inheritance in the land of promise would be lost along with God's covenant promise to be their God and the God of their children. By buying the parcel of land and restoring it to Elimelech's line, Boaz could ensure that Elimelech and Naomi's descendants would not lose their tangible connection to God himself.

Ruth continued to work in the barley fields throughout the harvesting season, and then Naomi determined it was time for Ruth to propose marriage to this potential family redeemer. That's what Ruth was doing when she went to the threshing floor in the middle of the night and lay down at Boaz's feet. When he woke up, she said to him, "Spread the corner of your covering over me, for you are my family redeemer" (Ruth 3:9). She was essentially saying to Boaz, "Will you marry me? Will you protect me? Will you provide for me?" Here was Ruth, a foreigner, and she was asking to become part of the covenant family, a fellow partaker of the promises of God.

Ruth went to the threshing floor with an empty future looming. She left with a promise from Boaz that he would do for her all that she had asked. She was going to be a bride. But there was a bit of a snag in the plan: Another family member was a closer relative, and Boaz had to give him the first opportunity to serve the family in this way. So Ruth left with a promise, and she also left with provision—six scoops of barley that Boaz gave to her, saying, "Don't go back to your mother-in-law empty-handed" (Ruth 3:17).

We have to wonder what Naomi heard when Ruth spoke of not coming back "empty-handed." It's as if the Lord were using her own words to remind her that he was not unaware of her emptiness. He was still the Lord of steadfast love. Naomi had come back to Bethlehem focused on the emptiness in her life, expecting only coldness from the God she thought had turned against her. But instead of coldness, she was experiencing kindness. Instead of remaining empty, her pantry, her stomach, her heart, and her life were being filled by God through Ruth and Boaz. As pastor David Helm says, "The seeds in Ruth's scarf that will fill Naomi's stomach hint at the seed that will fill Ruth's womb and redeem them both."[11]

Grace Begins to Work in Us

Boaz sent Ruth home with a preview, a down payment on all he intended to provide to Ruth and Naomi as their family redeemer. And in a sense, this is the point in the story where we find the most in common with these characters. We, too, have a promise from our Redeemer. We have heard him say to us, "I will redeem you," and that promise is everything to us. We're waiting for the wedding day, waiting for the consummation when everything that has been promised to us will become ours as we are covered by, joined to, saved by, and provided for by our Redeemer, Jesus.

We're waiting for the wedding day, waiting for the consummation when everything that has been promised to us will become ours as we are covered by, joined to, saved by, and provided for by our Redeemer, Jesus.

We are aware—sometimes acutely, painfully—that we haven't yet experienced everything that has been promised. There are still some empty places that haven't yet been filled. But we have the promise of an inheritance in the Promised Land of the new heaven and new earth. And we have the Spirit as a guarantee, a down payment on all of the riches we are set to inherit (see 2 Corinthians 1:22). In fact, we're beginning to enjoy them now in part. The Spirit is filling our lives with love, joy, peace, patience, kindness, goodness, gentleness, faithfulness, and self-control—fruit of his Spirit blossoming in our lives. But we don't yet have everything our Redeemer intends to provide to us. We know that the fullness promised to us in Christ is not a fullness of blessing in this age, but is largely reserved for the next. And here in the darkness of this life we often find ourselves longing for the dawn of that coming age.

When the unnamed closer relative who could have redeemed Elimelech's land found out that the deed for the land came with the obligation to marry Elimelech's widowed Moabite daughter-in-law, and that a son who came out of that union would inherit the land rather than it being added to his own holdings, he was no longer interested. So Boaz was free to redeem Ruth and Naomi, and he was glad to pay the cost to redeem them.

The story seems to come to a pleasing conclusion

when we read, "So Boaz took Ruth into his home, and she became his wife. When he slept with her, the LORD enabled her to become pregnant, and she gave birth to a son" (Ruth 4:13). Earlier we saw Ruth bring provision for Naomi out of her scarf filled with grain, and now we see Ruth bring provision for Naomi out of her womb. We see a radiant Naomi, surrounded by the women of the town, celebrating God's provision of a redeemer for her family and a child who, in a sense, brought her back to life, shaking off all of her bitterness. A child who would inherit Elimelech's land and provide for her in her old age.

"Naomi took the baby and cuddled him to her breast. And she cared for him as if he were her own" (Ruth 4:16). As we gaze into this final scene, we see that Naomi's arms were now full. Her heart was full. Her future was full. There was no way she would have wanted to be called Mara now. Instead of being called "Bitter," surely she wanted to be called "Beloved." Life had replaced death. Joy had replaced sorrow. Hope had replaced despair. Naomi had experienced the steadfast love of the Lord in such tangible ways.

Grace Changes the World

But the book of Ruth doesn't end with Naomi rocking a baby; it ends with a genealogy. And so we realize that this story is about more than Boaz meeting Ruth and Naomi's personal emptiness and need. It turns out that this story is really about God working through this needy family to meet a far greater need in the world. We read that they named Ruth and Boaz's baby Obed and that he became the father of Jesse and, ultimately, the grandfather of David.

The book of Ruth began with a reminder of the empty place in the lives of God's people. They had no king, and therefore everyone was doing what seemed right in their own eyes. God's people needed a leader, a king, who would lead them in the worship of God, who would defeat their enemies, who would rule in justice and righteousness. And through this union between Boaz and Ruth, through all of the difficult circumstances that brought them together, all of the emptiness and angst that seemed to Naomi to be signs of God's hand against her, God was actually at work providing what his people needed most—a king.

This king would establish the throne on which an even greater king, his greater son, would one day sit. One day, a son of David would be born in Bethlehem. He, too, would be a redeemer, a rescuer. He, too, would be willing to pay the cost to redeem not only those from the family but also those, like Ruth, who were outside the family. He would redeem people like you and me—people who were once strangers and for-eigners but who have been made citizens along with all of God's holy people, members of God's family (see Ephesians 2:19).

He left the far country of heaven, not to come to a land of plenty or a home where he would be welcomed. "He came to his own people, and even they rejected him" (John 1:11). On the cross, Jesus, unlike Naomi, really did experience having the hand of God turned against him. The Lord really did cause him to suffer. Isaiah writes, "It was the LORD's good plan to crush him and cause him grief" (53:10). There, on the cross, Jesus was purchasing our redemption. And as we come to him, asking to be covered by him and joined to him, we find that "from his fullness we have all received, grace upon grace" (John 1:16, ESV).

So this story leads us to ask ourselves some all-important questions: Have I ever turned away from the things and places and people I thought would provide me with life but have only left me empty? Have I ever truly turned toward the only one who can fill my life with his grace and goodness? Have I ever come and put myself at the feet of the Redeemer and asked him to cover me, care for me, bind himself to me, provide for me, protect me?

When we've been redeemed, welcomed into the

family, and provided for, we may still experience some emptiness, but we know it is not because God has turned against us. Rather, we can endure some emptiness, confident that our Redeemer will not ultimately fail us, confident that "if God is for us, who can ever be against us? Since he did not spare even his own Son but gave him up for us all, won't he also give us everything else?" (Romans 8:31-32).

My friend, if you are feeling tempted to have your needs met somewhere, anywhere away from God—somewhere forbidden, somewhere that promises life but only delivers death—I want to say to you, as I would have wanted to say to Elimelech and his little family as they packed their bags for Moab, "Don't do it! Don't go! Cry out to God in repentance! Cry out to God to send relief! Put your trust in God to save you and supply you with what you need. Don't seek out some solution apart from God, away from where he has promised to bless his people—which is in Christ alone." What may seem like a reasonable step for self-preservation will prove to provide no lasting preservation.

When all you can see are the empty places, put your confident hope in what you can't see. Put your hope in the God who is for you. God has not raised his fist against you; instead, God's hand is at work in your life. See that even the hardest providences of life come to us through our Redeemer's nail-scarred hands. He's allowing this emptiness in your life, seeking to draw you back to the place where he intends to bless you beyond what you can imagine. You just can't see it at this point in your story. Trust him to the end. He is guiding the story of your life toward restoration, toward redemption, toward resurrection.

Know that just as Boaz was drawn down into Ruth and Naomi's need, your Redeemer is drawn down into your need. Your desperate need is not evidence that he is against you but rather an opportunity for him to demonstrate the ways in which he is for you. He sees below the surface desires into your deeper and more significant needs. He may not fulfill every desire you see as a need from your limited perspective, but he is committed to meeting your true and deepest needs fully and forever.

> *Even the hardest providences of life come to us through our Redeemer's nail-scarred hands.*

Whatever it is that has carved out a huge cistern in your soul, God wants to fill your emptiness with his grace and kindness. Your Redeemer longs to take you under his wing and cover you with his robe, to protect you and provide for you. He has done what is necessary under the law to redeem you from your desperate situation and has paid the price required with his own blood. He will take you into his home. He will satisfy your hunger with himself because he is the Bread of Life. He will heal your heart, which has been broken by the sorrows and losses inflicted on it by life in this world. He will be kind to you. He will love you. He will share with you his own inheritance in the heavenly land. He will fill your future with all of the royal privileges of being in the family of Jesus Christ, the Son of David.

CHAPTER FOUR

A ROYAL TABLE

God Fills Our Emptiness with His Kindness

LIFE CAN CHANGE IN AN INSTANT. It can change with an unexpected phone call, a sudden move, a single decision, a simple conversation. Many of us can look back and identify the moment when the course of our lives was altered, for good or for bad. Sometimes it resulted from a choice we made or an action we took. Other times it was the choice someone else made—the choice to drink and drive, the choice to turn and leave, the choice to stay and fight—that changed everything. And sometimes there is no place or no person at which we can point the finger of blame or responsibility. It just happened. It just is.

Life in this broken world can be cruel. Relentlessly cruel.

The Cruelty of Mephibosheth's Life

Life was cruel to a little five-year-old boy named Mephibosheth. At first he had everything going for him. His grandfather was Saul, the mighty king of Israel, and his dad, Jonathan, was someone he could look up to and count on, a man who saw things as they really were and was willing to risk his life to do the right thing. Mephibosheth lived on the grand estate owned by the king. As a five-year-old boy he probably wasn't thinking about what he stood to inherit or the possibility that he himself might be king of Israel one day; he simply enjoyed his life of comfort in the home of the king.

But then in one day, everything changed. A report came in from Jezreel that the Philistines had attacked Israel, and many soldiers were slaughtered on the slopes of Mount Gilboa, including his father and many of his uncles. His grandfather Saul fell on his sword in disgrace. Not only did this leave Mephibosheth without a father and grandfather, it left him without a home. As a member of the royal family in a moment when the throne was threatened, his life was immediately in danger, so Mephibosheth's nurse grabbed him and fled to somewhere safe. But in the chaos and fear of the moment, she dropped him. He fell in such a way that both of his feet suffered permanent damage (see 2 Samuel 4:4).

In that one cruel day, Mephibosheth lost his father, his uncles, and his grandfather. In another sense he lost his future as a member of the royal family and even the possibility of one day sitting on the royal throne. He lost his home. And he also lost his ability to walk, which meant a loss of mobility, a loss of independence, and a loss of dignity.

A friend of the family took him in, but his living conditions changed significantly. This family friend, Makir, lived in Lo-debar. Lo-debar was likely a good place to live if you wanted to stay off the radar of anyone looking to make sure there were no living descendants of Saul, the former king. It wasn't just on the other side of the tracks; it was literally in the middle of nowhere. The capital of Nowheresville. The name of the place meant "no pasture." There was no place for cattle to graze, no place to plant crops. It was a rocky wilderness a long way from the lush gardens of the royal palace.

Mephibosheth was also a long way from his carefree days as a son of the future king. As he lived out his days in Lo-debar, his nights were likely restless. He was always listening for a knock on the door, convinced that his days were numbered. Lesson number one in royal rule is that when you become the king of a country, you wipe out all of the members of the previous royal family who might be a threat to your claim to the throne. So

Mephibosheth must have lived in constant fear of soldiers showing up in Lo-debar. For fifteen years or so, the knock never came. Nothing happened. Nobody visited Nowheresville.

But then one day, everything changed.

The Kindness of God to David

For a while after Saul died, the ten northern tribes had one of Mephibosheth's uncles, Ishbosheth, as their king, while David ruled over two tribes in the south. But Ishbosheth's rule came to a bitter end, and David became king over all twelve tribes. Once David took the fortress of Jebus, it became his royal city of Jerusalem. And when he determined to build a house for his God in the city where his own palace stood, God spoke to him through the prophet Nathan, telling him that he had very different plans. Instead of David building God a house, God intended to make David into a house. In other words, God intended for David's descendants to become an enduring dynasty. God promised David that one day one of his descendants would sit on his throne, ruling over a kingdom that would last forever.

God promised to show steadfast love—or, in the Hebrew, *hesed*—to David and his descendants. *Hesed* is one of those Hebrew terms that simply can't be captured by a single English word. Perhaps that is fitting, as what is being communicated is, in many ways, too magnificent to be captured in human language. It stands for a cluster of ideas—relentless and unlimited love, mercy, grace, and kindness. This steadfast or loyal love is essential to God's very character. It's at the center of how he introduced himself to Moses when he said, "The LORD, the LORD, a God merciful and gracious, slow to anger, and *abounding in steadfast love* and faithfulness, keeping *steadfast love* for thousands" (Exodus 34:6-7, ESV, italics added).

David was overwhelmed by the steadfast love of the Lord that came to him in the form of this incredible promise. He also experienced this steadfast love as the Lord gave him victory over his enemies. But David didn't only want to be a recipient of God's kindness to him; he wanted to become a conduit of that kindness. The gracious covenant that God made with David evidently got him thinking about the covenant he had made many years before with his soul-brother, Jonathan. Jonathan, the son of Saul and most likely the future king, had known that God had chosen David to be king over Israel, and that Samuel had anointed him. In submission to God and as an act of friendship toward David, Jonathan had given his royal robe and armor to David, covenanting with him that David would, in fact, be the future king. Jonathan said to

David, "May the LORD be with you as he used to be with my father. And may you treat me with the faithful love of the LORD as long as I live. But if I die, treat my family with this faithful love, even when the LORD destroys all your enemies from the face of the earth" (1 Samuel 20:13-15).

David's experience of God's kindness in the promises made to him, combined with his remembrance of the promises he made to Jonathan to treat Jonathan's family with the same kind of God-like lovingkindness, motivated David to ask a question in his royal court. And in that instant, though Mephibosheth knew nothing about it, everything began to change in his life.

> One day David asked, "Is anyone in Saul's family still alive—anyone to whom I can show kindness for Jonathan's sake?" He summoned a man named Ziba, who had been one of Saul's servants. "Are you Ziba?" the king asked.
>
> "Yes sir, I am," Ziba replied.
>
> The king then asked him, "Is anyone still alive from Saul's family? If so, I want to show God's kindness to them."
>
> Ziba replied, "Yes, one of Jonathan's sons is still alive. He is crippled in both feet."
>
> "Where is he?" the king asked.

"In Lo-debar," Ziba told him, "at the home of Makir son of Ammiel."

2 SAMUEL 9:1-4

Out of the overflow of kindness he had received from God, David wanted to show kindness to someone else. But he was not interested in doing some sort of "random act of kindness." No, this was much deeper and far more significant. He said specifically that he wanted to show *God's kindness* to any living member of Saul's family. God-style commitment to that person's good is what David had in mind. It would be risky. It was going to cost him. People might think he was a little crazy. But he didn't care.

David put no qualifiers on his question. He didn't ask, "Is there anyone who is worthy, anyone trustworthy, anyone who deserves this kind of kindness?" even though by mentioning Mephibosheth's disability, Ziba seemed to be hinting that Mephibosheth might not look good in the court of the king. What David had in mind was God-like kindness that is lavished on those who don't deserve it, those who have done nothing to earn it, those who have nothing but need to offer.

When you and I become aware of how much kindness we've received from God, when we savor it instead of taking it for granted, it changes us. It changes our perspective. It changes our interactions. Instead of always being so concerned about how we are being treated, how we are being included, how our needs are being met, we're increasingly concerned about how others are being treated, whether or not they are being included, whether or not their needs are being met. We're able to look up from our own circumstances and situations and begin asking the question, "Whom can I show kindness to?" We find that the place inside us that once seemed so empty has become a reservoir for kindness that overflows onto the people around us. That feeling of being a nobody in a world of somebodies isn't so acute, so dominating anymore, because we're simply too busy caring about other people. Those tendencies to wallow in self-pity when life is cruel don't have as much pull as they used to because as we are involved in the lives of others, the hurts of others, we find ourselves constantly and increasingly grateful for what God has given to us, what he's done for us through Christ, and what he is doing in us by his Spirit.

When you and I become aware of how much kindness we've received from God, when we savor it instead of take it for granted, it changes us.

The Kindness of David to Mephibosheth

Mephibosheth had spent years dreading the day when David's soldiers would knock on his door. And finally that day came.

> So David sent for him and brought him from Makir's home. His name was Mephibosheth; he was Jonathan's son and Saul's grandson. When he came to David, he bowed low to the ground in deep respect. David said, "Greetings, Mephibosheth."
>
> Mephibosheth replied, "I am your servant."
>
> 2 SAMUEL 9:5-6

Mephibosheth must have come limping or on crutches into the presence of the king. With his disability it must have been difficult or perhaps uncomfortable to bow low to the ground before David. Perhaps his eyes were squeezed shut in anticipation of a sword coming down on his neck. But instead, words of kindness, promises of provision, and assurances of a future fell on his ears.

> "Don't be afraid!" David said. "I intend to show kindness to you because of my promise to your father, Jonathan. I will give you all the property

that once belonged to your grandfather
Saul, and you will eat here with me at the
king's table!"

2 SAMUEL 9:7

Mephibosheth could hardly believe his ears at this
turnaround. He had been falling all of his life. He fell
from his nurse's arms at the age of five and then fell into
seclusion, insecurity, and insignificance in Lo-debar.
What a fall from grace. But then he came and fell on
his face before the king. And instead of ending up at the
other end of a sword, Mephibosheth found that he had
fallen once again. This time, he had fallen *into* grace.[12]

This grace came to Mephibosheth because of a
promise—a promise David made many years before to
Mephibosheth's father, that he would show kindness to
his children. As David rolled out the ways in which he
intended to show this kindness, it began to dawn on
Mephibosheth that this was going to change everything
about his life. David's promises were not token kindnesses; these were pervasive, ongoing kindnesses.

A place to call home. David told Mephibosheth that
he was going to give him all the property that had
belonged to his grandfather Saul. We might easily rush
through this point, but imagine how much property
Saul, the first king of Israel, must have acquired over the

many years of his reign. Years earlier, when the people of Israel had asked for a king, the prophet Samuel had warned them that a king would take and take and take from them, including taking their property for himself. So when David promised to give Mephibosheth all the land that once belonged to Saul, surely it was a grand estate. Think Downton Abbey or Biltmore Estate, or the Ponderosa Ranch (and yes, I realize I'm dating myself with that one).

Mephibosheth, who had been hiding out in a hovel in Lo-debar, was changing addresses. And in his becoming owner of the land, his fortune changed significantly. In the ancient world, land was the measure of wealth. In this one day, Mephibosheth became a wealthy man. He not only had land, he had a staff of servants to work the land and mind the cattle. David assigned Ziba, along with his fifteen sons and twenty servants, to farm the land. No longer would Mephibosheth live in the land of nothing with nothing. He was going to have a place to call home, a share in the land of promise, an inheritance to pass along to his children.

A place at the king's table. In giving Mephibosheth a home of his own, David was not sending him away. Far from it. Instead, he was making Mephibosheth part of the family. He wanted Mephibosheth to come in close. He wanted to know him, share life with him. He wanted to see him every night at the dinner table and hear about his day. "You will eat here with me at the king's table," David told Mephibosheth (2 Samuel 9:7).

Imagine what Mephibosheth's diet had been like living in "no pasture." Now imagine what it meant to eat at the king's table. Imagine the bounty; imagine the grandeur; imagine the guests, the conversation. The food at this table was going to be good, but the fellowship would be even better. Mephibosheth had been without a family for so long, and now he was being adopted into the king's family. We read, "And from that time on, Mephibosheth ate regularly at David's table, like one of the king's own sons" (2 Samuel 9:11). He'd been an enemy of the state, and now he'd become an adopted son of the king. He'd been so alone, and now he had a place of belonging. He didn't have to be afraid anymore. He didn't have to hide anymore. The kindness of the king had undone the lifetime of cruelties he had experienced.

The Kindness of the King to You and Me

Just as life changed in a moment for Mephibosheth, so life changed in an instant for a young woman living many years later in Nazareth. The angel Gabriel told her that she was going to have a son. "He will be very great and will be called the Son of the Most High. The Lord God will give him the throne of his ancestor David.

And he will reign over Israel forever; his Kingdom will never end!" (Luke 1:32-33).

So what kind of king was this Son of the Most High? He was kind. "A vast crowd brought to him people who were lame, blind, crippled, those who couldn't speak, and many others. They laid them before Jesus, and he healed them all" (Matthew 15:30).

We get a sense of the heart of King Jesus in the story he told about a man who was preparing a great feast. He sent out invitations for the banquet, but the invitees began making excuses for why they would not come. So he sent his servant into the streets and alleys of the town to invite the poor, the crippled, the blind, and the lame.

When you read about these people, maybe your first thought is that Jesus was describing somebody else. You may have your struggles, but you certainly don't see yourself in the category of poor, crippled, blind, or lame. But "lame" is one way the Bible describes the spiritual condition of every person apart from an encounter with Jesus. We can't come to him unless he draws us to himself. We're poor, with nothing to offer. We're blind. We can't see him until he reveals himself to us. None of us stride with self-confidence into the presence of our King. We all limp our way in.

And none of us deserve to get in. In fact, we deserve just the opposite. We deserve to be treated as enemies because that's what we were. It was when "we were ene- mies we were reconciled to God by the death of his Son" (Romans 5:10, ESV). If you are joined to Christ by faith, it is because God sought you out when you were hiding from him, when you were his enemy. He came looking for you out of a desire to show his loving-kindness to you because of the covenant he made before the foundations of the world. "Even before he made the world, God loved us and chose us in Christ to be holy and without fault in his eyes. God decided in advance to adopt us into his own family by bringing us to himself through Jesus Christ. . . . He has showered his kindness on us, along with all wisdom and understanding" (Ephesians 1:4-5, 8).

None of us stride with self-confidence into the presence of our King. We all limp our way in.

On the night before he was crucified, King Jesus summoned his family to the table. But this was like no previous Passover meal.

Jesus said, "I have been very eager to eat this Passover meal with you before my suffering begins. For I tell you now that I won't eat this meal again until its meaning is fulfilled in the Kingdom of God."

Then he took a cup of wine and gave thanks to God for it. Then he said, "Take this and share it among yourselves. For I will not drink wine again until the Kingdom of God has come."

He took some bread and gave thanks to God for it. Then he broke it in pieces and gave it to the disciples, saying, "This is my body, which is given for you. Do this in remembrance of me."

After supper he took another cup of wine and said, "This cup is the new covenant between God and his people—an agreement confirmed with my blood, which is poured out as a sacrifice for you."

LUKE 22:15-20

Our King has summoned us to his table. He's calling us to feed on his atoning death as our life. He's calling us to drink in his salvation benefits. As we regularly share a meal at the Lord's Table with our brothers and sisters, we find that our hearts' longing for belonging is being met. We're strengthened for serving others rather than being so concerned about being served. We're strengthened to ask the question "Is there anyone I can show kindness to for Christ's sake and for his honor and glory?"

We're also strengthened for the waiting. When we follow Jesus as our King, it doesn't mean that we can expect to receive an estate or servants or a seat at the best of tables in the immediate present. It doesn't mean our crippling injuries will be immediately healed or that the hurts of the past will be easily forgotten. At least not yet.

Life can be cruel. It can leave us crippled by financial catastrophe, crippled by difficult circumstances, crippled by the cutting words of someone whose opinion mattered. But God has not abandoned us to the cruelty of life in this world under a curse. He has not forgotten us. He has not forgotten his covenant promise to show loving-kindness. He is, even now, seeking out those he can show his kindness to. If you have so far lingered away from his presence, hear him say to you, "You don't have anything to be afraid of in my presence. On the cross, my Son, Jesus, became my enemy so you could be my friend. He was put out of the family so you could be adopted into it. He feasted on my wrath and anger so that you can feast forever on my love and mercy."

My friend, if you have come before this King and bowed before him in humility, realizing that you have nothing but need to offer to him, the day is coming when everything about your life will change. It will happen in a moment, in the blink of an eye: Our King will come for us. The greater David is going to spread a table at which we'll be welcomed to sit and feast forever.

Perhaps you sit alone tonight. Perhaps you see yourself as nobody living a nothing life in Nowheresville. I want you to know that the day will come when you will be gathered with a multitude of brothers and sisters. There will be a place for you to call home, a place for you at the table. Jesus said, "Many Gentiles will come from all over the world—from east and west—and sit down with Abraham, Isaac, and Jacob at the feast in the Kingdom of Heaven" (Matthew 8:11). This is the expansive nature of our King's kindness.

God has not forgotten you. More significantly, he has not forgotten his covenant, made before you were born—before the foundations of the world—to show his loving-kindness to you.

God has not forgotten you. More significantly, he has not forgotten his covenant, made before you were born—before the foundations of the world—to show his loving-kindness to you. When you were not looking for him, when you were hiding from him, fearful that any interaction with him would only add to your shame, he sought you out to draw you to himself, saying, "Don't be afraid! I intend to show kindness to you because of my promise to Abraham, your father. I will give you a place to call home, an inheritance in my heavenly land, and there, you will eat with me at the King's table in a heavenly banquet that will never end."

CHAPTER FIVE

AN UNQUENCHABLE THIRST

God Fills Our Emptiness with His Life

"THE END" SEEMS TO APPEAR on the screen at the most convenient point in romantic comedies. It comes as the crisis is averted and the couple realizes they want to spend the rest of their lives together in what they—and we, as the viewers—expect is going to be perfect bliss. How convenient that the story stops there. Imagine if the cameras kept rolling on some of our favorite movie couples as they began to live out their lives together. I'm not sure things would always be as smooth as the happily-ever-after endings suggest.

Yes, we swoon when Tom Cruise, in the movie *Jerry Maguire*, interrupts an evening Renée Zellweger is having with her girlfriends and says, "You . . . complete

. . . me." But do we really think a marriage relationship between the uber-ambitious sports agent and his former secretary is going to be able to weather Jerry's being away from home so much during the football season?

Yes, we are relieved when Billy Crystal, playing Harry Burns in *When Harry Met Sally*, says to Meg Ryan, playing Sally Albright, "I came here tonight because when you realize you want to spend the rest of your life with somebody, you want the rest of your life to start as soon as possible." But do we really think marriage between Harry, with all of his bad habits, and Sally, with all of her high-maintenance idiosyncrasies, is going to be smooth sailing?

Yes, we feel hope when Julia Roberts, playing the movie star Anna Scott in *Notting Hill*, says to Hugh Grant, playing bookstore owner William Thacker, "I'm just a girl standing in front of a boy, asking him to love her." As the closing credits roll over a pregnant Anna reading a book on a park bench with her *Horse and Hound* reporter impersonator husband, we have all kinds of hopes for this marriage. But do we really think the fame and financial gap between them isn't going to be a constant rub?

Romantic movies simply don't have to show the ongoing reality of two imperfect, often self-centered people dealing with the challenges of daily life together over the long haul. Films conveniently end when it seems as if the couple is going to be happy forever.

But we who live in the real world know that life and love simply do not always work out the way they do in the movies. We know that we're not perfect and that there are no perfect people out there to be married to. There are not, and have never been, perfect marriages untouched by things such as disappointment, boredom, betrayal, financial pressure, catastrophe, illness, dysfunction, divorce, or death.

We still hope, though. We still have high expectations for our romantic relationships, thinking that if we can just find and keep the right person, or change the person or the relationship we have, then we will be happy. Then we won't feel so empty.

But here is where God has the opportunity to go to work in our lives. God does some of his best work in our longings to be loved. You see, you and I were never meant to gaze forever into the eyes of another human being and find in him or her all we need. In fact, no human relationship, no matter how emotionally intense, can fill up the empty place in our lives that only our heavenly husband can fill.

God does some of his best work in our longings to be loved.

Thirsty in Judah

From the beginning, the Bible describes God's relationship with his people, the nation of Israel, in terms of marriage—a marriage in which God intended to satisfy the desires of his bride and capture her heart. "For your Creator will be your husband," God said to Israel through the prophet Isaiah. But sadly, the marriage between God and his bride, Israel, which started out with great promise, went very wrong. Through the prophet Jeremiah, we hear the Lord wistfully remembering how his love story with his people began:

> This is what the LORD says:
>
> "I remember how eager you were to please me
>   as a young bride long ago,
> how you loved me and followed me
>   even through the barren wilderness."
>
> JEREMIAH 2:2

It's as if God is looking at his album of wedding photos and he sees a picture of his bride, Israel, when their love was new. She loved him and was eager to please him, willing to follow him into the wilderness on their way from Egypt to the Promised Land. Two million people walked through the wilderness, where there were no natural springs or flowing rivers. There, Israel's holy husband opened up a spring of water that came gushing out of a rock for them to drink. It was early in this marriage, and he wanted them to see that he was going to be the source of what would satisfy them.

We most often think of thirst as the physical sensation of needing or wanting to drink something. But we also use the term figuratively, as when we speak of having a thirst for knowledge. To thirst for something is to desire it strongly, and we see that meaning in the Bible as well. In fact, throughout the Bible's story, the imagery of thirst and water is used in connection with desire.

There in the wilderness, God had made it clear that he wanted to be the focus of his people's affections. His number one commandment to them was "You must not have any other god but me. You must not make for yourself an idol of any kind, or an image of anything in the heavens or on the earth or in the sea. You must not bow down to them or worship them, for I, the LORD your God, am a jealous God who will not tolerate your affection for any other gods" (Deuteronomy 5:7-9).

But over time Israel repeatedly proved unfaithful, giving her affections to all sorts of other gods. The Lord gave her a book of love poetry—the Song of Solomon— meant to show her how passionate he intended his relationship with her to be. He sent a prophet, Hosea, who demonstrated how persistent God intended to be in loving Israel despite her unfaithfulness. But she persisted in her liaisons with other gods at the altars built in the hills surrounding Jerusalem, even though it only left her empty.

> Thus says the LORD,
> "What injustice did your fathers find in Me,
> That they went far from Me
> And walked after emptiness and became empty?"
> JEREMIAH 2:5, NASB

The gods they worshiped were empty, unreal, and worthless, and the people became like the gods they worshiped—empty. They thought that they were merely adding a little worship of these other gods to their ongoing worship of the one true God. But God is a jealous God who does not share the affection of his people with other gods.

> For my people have done two evil things:
> They have abandoned me—
>   the fountain of living water.
> And they have dug for themselves cracked cisterns
>   that can hold no water at all!
>
> JEREMIAH 2:13

Notice that Jeremiah calls two things evil—abandoning God and trying to find refreshment from other gods. We don't think of abandoning an intimate relationship with God as evil. Instead, we consider it harmless drifting or a stint of being too busy or distracted—if we think of it as a problem at all. And we certainly don't use the word *evil* to describe so many things that fill our lives in the place that should have been reserved for God. In fact, on the surface, the things we fill our lives with may not be bad at all. The problem comes as we grow to want them more than we want Christ, as we grow to love them more than we love Christ.

God's perspective, according to Jeremiah, is that it is actually a great evil when we prefer something other than God himself as the source of what fills our lives with joy. It is wrong, and not merely a bad habit, to approach each day seeking to savor the taste of something we find in this world—be it a substance, an experience, or a person—while starving ourselves of the companionship of God. Evidently it breaks the heart of God when we prefer to sip on the things this world offers while refusing to drink from the fountain he provides, having no taste for, no appetite for him.

And how do we know if this is true for us? Perhaps one way to do a check on our hearts is to use the Psalm 73 test. Psalm 73:25-26 reads,

Whom have I in heaven but you?
    I desire you more than anything on earth.
My health may fail, and my spirit may grow weak,
    but God remains the strength of my heart;
    he is mine forever.

Can you imagine yourself being able to say these words of the psalmist to God and really mean them? Is there anyone or anything that would keep you from saying that the one thing you desire more than anything on earth is God himself? If those closest to you were to identify what animates your life, what you talk about most and arrange your schedule to enjoy most, what would it be? Your favorite sports team? Your favorite hobby? Your political party? Your professional pursuits?

Anyone or anything that rivals the place that belongs to God alone is the well you have dug for yourself to drink from. And eventually you will discover that this well, this cistern, is cracked and broken.

Anyone or anything that rivals the place that belongs to God alone is the well you have dug for yourself to drink from. And eventually you will discover that this well, this cistern, is cracked and broken. It won't hold water.

It can't contain all of your expectations. Ultimately it will be unable to deliver the happiness and security and life you crave.

That career trajectory you think is watertight if you keep working hard? It's broken. It cannot deliver the satisfaction you think it can. That perfect family that will fill your life with joy into old age? There's a crack in this cistern you can't see at this point. That lifestyle you're building one paycheck at a time? It won't be enough to bring you contentment. The health or beauty you're working every day to maintain? It won't last long enough.

The people Jeremiah was prophesying to, the two tribes of the southern kingdom of Judah, had already witnessed what happened when the ten tribes of the northern kingdom refused to abandon their idols in order to worship God alone. God had used the nation of Assyria to put an end to their idolatry. The Assyrians swept into Israel, carrying the people away and scattering them throughout all of the lands Assyria had conquered. Then the Assyrians imported other conquered peoples into Israel, and they brought their own gods with them. They intermarried with the few Israelites who were left behind on the land, and their descendants were the mixed-race people who were so hated by Israelites in Jesus' day—the Samaritans.

It is one of these Samaritans the New Testament introduces us to in the book of John. And she was thirsty. So very thirsty to be loved.

Thirsty at the Well

It was the middle of the day, and she had made the trek to the well to get water. She was going in the heat of the day, the time when most of the other women of the town avoided making the labor-intensive, heatstroke-inducing trip. But this woman was willing to bear the load in the heat because she simply didn't want to face all the other women in town—for reasons that become clear in the conversation to come.

When she got to the well, there was a Jewish man there who asked her to give him a drink of water. Everything about this was wrong. She was a Samaritan and he was a Jew. Samaritans and Jews didn't talk to each other, let alone share a drinking cup. She expressed her shock at his request, and his response brought not only another shock, but also some confusion.

> Jesus replied, "If you only knew the gift God has for you and who you are speaking to, you would ask me, and I would give you living water."
>
> JOHN 4:10

A gift God has for me? If I only knew who I was speaking to? Living water?

Samaritans had the law of Moses but not the rest of the Old Testament. So it's possible the woman was unfamiliar with Jeremiah's writings in which God had described himself as the fountain of living water. But she would have been well aware of the story of her ancestors in the wilderness who drank water from a rock that Moses had struck with his staff. So perhaps this metaphor of "living water" rang a bell for her. Perhaps she was aware that when this stranger spoke of drinking from a well he was using the intimate language of personal love drawn from the Old Testament, a metaphor for marriage or a sexual relationship. Or perhaps she was willfully dull regarding this offer of spiritual rather than physical drink. All she could seem to think about was her bucket and her thirst.

> "But sir, you don't have a rope or a bucket," she said, "and this well is very deep. Where would you get this living water?" . . .
>
> Jesus replied, "Anyone who drinks this water will soon become thirsty again. But those who drink the water I give will never be thirsty again. It becomes a fresh, bubbling spring within them, giving them eternal life."
>
> JOHN 4:11, 13-14

Perhaps the promise of eternal life hits us as something we may need in the future, but not something we need now. We're fixated on what we see as our urgent need in the present, and talk of eternal life can sound otherworldly or escapist. But Jesus was not merely speaking about a quantity or length of the life we have now; he was speaking of a quality of life that surpasses even what was experienced in Eden. The woman, though, still didn't get it.

> "Please, sir," the woman said, "give me this water! Then I'll never be thirsty again, and I won't have to come here to get water."
> JOHN 4:15

Jesus was not offering her water she could drink with a cup; he was offering water she could drink with her heart. He was offering her a relationship that would satisfy her and provide her the life and love she craved. He could see that, like her ancestors, she had abandoned the fountain of living water and dug for herself a cistern that wouldn't hold any water. So he helped her to see how broken her cistern really was.

> "Go and get your husband," Jesus told her.
> "I don't have a husband," the woman replied.

Jesus said, "You're right! You don't have a husband—for you have had five husbands, and you aren't even married to the man you're living with now. You certainly spoke the truth!"

JOHN 4:16-18

This woman's life had been one long series of unfulfilled dreams—wedding day after wedding day after wedding day. With each new man she met she had raised hopes, great plans, eager anticipation, and initial joy, which sooner or later descended into gradual disillusionment, desperate disappointment, eventual failure, and finally despair.

Every time she met another man and experienced the tingle of attraction, she hoped that he might be her source of living water, that he might fill her up in the way she longed to be filled. Maybe her five husbands had all been bad men who simply left her after using her. Or maybe one or more of them had been good men who just couldn't provide her with the fulfillment she expected from them. Perhaps her expectations and demands became unbearable. As Rico Tice said in a sermon, "It puts a terrible strain on any human being to be expected to quench another person's thirst for living water."[13]

No doubt the words of this man at the well sent a

surge of shame through the woman. But he wasn't trying to shame her. He was trying to help her see the thirst in her life that was even more significant than her physical thirst. She was thirsty to be known and loved, thirsty for life the way God originally intended it to be. She had an unquenchable thirst to be satisfied beyond a moment of pleasure, to be accepted and nurtured and cherished.

And here stood Jesus, offering her the water that would quench the inner thirst that all of her relationships had been unable to satisfy.

Jesus comes to each of us and says, "Come to me and drink. Discover that I am the only one who can quench your thirst."

I have to pause in this story to invite you to evaluate your own thirst. Have you been looking for a person to fulfill you in the way that only God can? Do you find yourself moving from one thing to another, trying to fill the void? Jumping from one relationship to another? From one job to the next? From one vacation to the next? Jesus comes to each of us and says, "Come to me and drink. Discover that I am the only one who can quench your thirst."

Thirsty at the Feast

A short time later, it was the Festival of Shelters, the time when faithful Jews from all over the known world converged on the capital city of Jerusalem. Every morning during the festival, the high priest would fill a pitcher with water from the fountain of Gihon, which supplied water for the pool of Siloam. As he filled it, the people sang, "With joy you will drink deeply from the fountain of salvation!" (Isaiah 12:3). Then the priest would lead the procession of people to the Temple, where he would pour out his pitcher of water onto the altar. This annual ritual reminded the people of that time when living water flowed out of the rock to quench the terrible thirst of their ancestors in the wilderness. But it also pointed the people forward toward the day the prophets Zechariah and Ezekiel wrote about, when life-giving, healing water would flow from the Temple of Jerusalem, becoming a river too deep to walk through. "Life will flourish wherever this water flows," Ezekiel wrote (47:9; see also Zechariah 14:8). As the people celebrated this festival, they anticipated the day when living water would flow from the Temple in Jerusalem throughout the entire world.

Try to picture in your mind the crowds of people gathered in Jerusalem for this festival. Imagine the water being drawn, carried, and then poured on the altar of the Temple. And then imagine what it must have been like to hear Jesus' voice echo through the crowd.

On the last day, the climax of the festival, Jesus
stood and shouted to the crowds, "Anyone
who is thirsty may come to me! Anyone who
believes in me may come and drink!

JOHN 7:37-38

What an invitation! Open to anyone who is thirsty.
Open to anyone who believes in him. It's an open invitation to put our heads down into the refreshing waters
that are only found in him and drink. Jesus says that
when we believe in him, the Holy Spirit is given to us,
and he begins to generate in us the kind of life we were
created for.

But to pour out this living water, Jesus had to die.
Just as Moses struck the rock in the wilderness with
the rod of judgment so that water flowed out for the
people to drink, so Jesus was struck with the rod of
God's judgment on the cross. And when he was struck,
living water flowed out so that people like me and you
can drink and drink and drink.

Jesus cried out from the cross, "I am thirsty" (John
19:28). He experienced the agonizing thirst that you
and I deserve to experience forever, so that you and I
can be satisfied forever. His tongue stuck to the roof
of his mouth and he was laid in the dust of death (see
Psalm 22:15) so that you and I will be able to drink in

the refreshing waters of the Holy Spirit and be raised to glorious life.

So let me ask you: Are you a drinker? That's what it means to be a Christian. It's not so much about a one-time religious experience or decision. It's about whether you have a thirst for God, and if so, whether you are drinking day by day from the fountain that is Christ. Or is the reality of your life that you might take a sip of Christ every once in a while, but you're really filling up your soul from some other cistern? At this point, perhaps the supply in the cistern you've built is sufficient. Perhaps it tastes sweet. But the truth is, it won't last. No other source can provide the life that Christ provides. Every other source will eventually dry up. And when it does, you will die of spiritual thirst.

Thirsty No More

But you don't have to die of thirst. Just as Jesus offered living water to that Samaritan woman at the well, and to the Jewish crowds gathered for the festival in Jerusalem, so Jesus offers himself to you as living water today. In fact, that's how the Bible ends—with an open invitation to thirsty people to come and drink.

> The Spirit and the bride say, "Come." Let
> anyone who hears this say, "Come." Let anyone

> who is thirsty come. Let anyone who desires
> drink freely from the water of life.
> REVELATION 22:17

You don't have to spend the rest of your life searching for someone who will satisfy your deep need to be loved. Instead, as you drink from the fountain of living water, you can expect to experience ongoing satisfaction, even as you anticipate the ultimate, unending satisfaction that is to come when the promises described in the book of Revelation become the reality we will live in forever.

> They will never again be hungry or thirsty;
>> they will never be scorched by the heat of the
>> sun.
> For the Lamb on the throne
>> will be their Shepherd.
> He will lead them to springs of life-giving water.
>> And God will wipe every tear from their eyes.
> REVELATION 7:16-17

My friend, the day is coming when the shadow of temporary human marriage will give way to the substance—the eternal marriage between Christ and his bride. And this will be the happiest, most satisfying marriage of all time. Until then, we simply can't expect any human to fill us up completely. No human relationship, no matter how good, can bear the weight of our expectations of complete satisfaction, perfect harmony, and intimacy that only this ultimate and eternal marriage will provide. Instead, our less-than-perfect marriages or our longings to be married can serve to keep us thirsty for this perfect marriage to come. We can expect God to be at work in our emptiness to woo us to himself.

Whether we're married or single, divorced or widowed, our lives are meant to be spent nurturing our longing for this better marriage. And someday that longing will be fulfilled. Don't stuff down those desires to be loved in this way; *direct your desires* toward the only one who can love you this way forever.[14]

CHAPTER SIX

A VANISHING BREATH

God Fills Our Emptiness with Meaning

WHY DO WE love websites like Rotten Tomatoes and TripAdvisor? Why do we read book reviews on Amazon and restaurant reviews on Yelp? Because we want to get some straightforward feedback from someone who has seen the movie, stayed in the hotel, read the book, or eaten at the restaurant. We want to gain some insight into what to expect, what to avoid, and what to enjoy from someone who has experience.

In a sense, that's what the book of Ecclesiastes offers to those of us who are willing to slog through its sometimes confusing, even depressing twelve chapters. Perhaps one way to take in what this book of ancient wisdom has to offer is to think of ourselves sitting across the table from the author at a coffee shop. This won't be a casual conversation. We're considering the deepest things of life.

However, it would seem that we're not sitting with the person who has written the review of life that makes up the bulk of the book, but rather with the narrator who sets up the reviewer at the beginning of the book and then comments on his review at the end. Ecclesiastes seems to open and close with a narrator who tells us what another person has searched out and reported on, and who then adds his own conclusion. We'll call this narrator our mentor, and we'll call the person who wrote his review of life under the sun *Q*, short for *Qoheleth*, which means "teacher" or "convener," the Hebrew name or title used for this person in Ecclesiastes. (And we'll do our best to live with there being no *u* after the *q* in his name.)

Our mentor, the narrator, begins by briefly quoting Q's conclusion and then sets up the questions that will be considered through the rest of the book.

> "Everything is meaningless," says the Teacher,
> "completely meaningless!"
>   What do people get for all their hard
> work under the sun? Generations come and
> generations go, but the earth never changes.

The sun rises and the sun sets, then hurries
around to rise again. The wind blows south,
and then turns north. Around and around it
goes, blowing in circles. Rivers run into the
sea, but the sea is never full. Then the water
returns again to the rivers and flows out again
to the sea. Everything is wearisome beyond
description. No matter how much we see, we
are never satisfied. No matter how much we
hear, we are not content.

ECCLESIASTES 1:2-8

Dissatisfaction, discontentment, boredom, relentless cycles of coming up short. These are the things that
have sent Q on his search. And they sound incredibly
familiar, don't they? Sometimes I feel as if my life is
a bottomless pit of desires that are never fully satisfied. When we read about Q's experience with life and
his search for answers, we're immediately interested
in his findings because we experience these very same
things.

Following this introduction, our mentor takes
eleven chapters to relate to us Q's experience-based
insight into what to expect, what to avoid, and what to
enjoy during the years we spend on this earth between
birth and death.

Q's Review of Life: Meaningless

As our mentor starts relating Q's careful review of life "under the sun," we learn at the outset that Q isn't simply speaking to us about life as a casual observer. Instead, Q says, "I devoted myself to search for understanding and to explore by wisdom everything being done under heaven" (1:13). This was an intense search, a thorough exploration and investigation. Q devoted himself to the all-important task of trying to make sense of life in this world, and the headline to his review is "Everything is meaningless, completely meaningless!" (see 1:2; 12:8). Q seems to be saying that our lives are like puffs of smoke, like warm breath on a cold day that vanishes quickly, has no permanent impact, and makes no lasting impression.

This does not exactly sound like good news for those of us who are looking for something to fill the emptiness in our lives. And then it seems to get worse as he continues:

I observed everything going on under the sun, and really, it is all meaningless—like chasing the wind.

What is wrong cannot be made right.
What is missing cannot be recovered.

1:14-15

The first thing Q seems to be saying is this:

When life doesn't seem to be working, it's not that you're not doing it right, it's that the world isn't right.

We can't read Q's words without thinking about the fact that there was a time when everything in the world was right, a time before everything went so terribly wrong. There was a time when the whole of humanity (which was Adam and Eve at that point) lived life "under the sun" (in Eden at that point) and had lives filled with purpose and meaning. Their relationship was untouched by conflict, they had no cause for shame, and their work was fulfilling. But that all ended when Adam and Eve listened to the evil serpent instead of obeying God. And when they sinned, the impact of that sin infiltrated and corrupted the entire creation. Adam and Eve's relationship with each other went from one flesh to fractured; their relationship with God went from intimate to estranged. Their work lives went from fulfilling to frustrating. Their future went from the anticipation of glory to the dread of death.

As much as we might hate to hear how messed up this world is, it is good for us to embrace this reality, because doing so has the power to save us from unrealistic expectations that life is somehow going to be different from this for us. Embracing this reality keeps us from being shocked when accidents happen and bodies age and relationships rupture. We often react to the nonsensical suffering inherent in this life as if something out of the ordinary and unexpected has happened. But Q seems to be saying that we should *expect* that life in this world will be difficult and disordered.

You and I should expect unexplainable, unexpected, even seemingly unbearable things to happen to us—things that don't happen on our schedule, things that don't make any sense, things that bring the brokenness of the world into the interior of our lives. We need to hear this because we are resistant to this wisdom; we reject this reality. We think that if we just have the right attitude and do the right things, then a life of ongoing comfort, uninterrupted satisfaction, and achieving our "destiny" is attainable.

We need to hear what Q is telling us because we think that if we can do this thing called life right . . .

if we can find and keep the job we were made for

if we can find and keep the spouse who was made for us

if we can conceive and raise the right number of healthy, easy-to-manage children

if we can make enough money to afford the house, the car, the education, and the vacations we want

if we can surround ourselves with a community
    who will add to rather than take from us
if we can accomplish the goals we aspire to
    then we'll be happy
    then we'll be satisfied
    then we won't have this nagging sense of . . .
        not having enough
        not doing enough
        not experiencing enough
        not being loved enough
        not being enough.

But that just isn't true.

There's something about the condition of this world that keeps us from experiencing a lasting sense of satisfaction. It's as if there is a crack at the center of the universe that runs through the center of our souls so that any sense of satisfaction we do attain slowly seeps out. It doesn't last.

- Someone pays us a generous compliment and it pleases us deep on the inside. But then someone else has a teeny-weeny criticism or doesn't notice us, and the satisfaction of the affirmation dissipates quickly.

- We finally get that thing we've researched and worked for—the new house, the new car, the new couch, the new nose, the new spouse—and before we know it, it just isn't enough. We start dreaming about something better.
- We spend a lifetime saving carefully toward a particular goal, and our funds are stolen by an unscrupulous money manager or lost in a failed investment.
- We finally retire, looking forward to traveling and enjoying life with our spouse—and then we lose him or her and must face the end of life alone.

About now you're beginning to think that this chapter is really turning negative, that there are plenty of other gurus out there who would be happy to tell you that if you have enough faith, if you take the right steps, if you pray the right prayers, then everything will turn around. Your relationships will be righted, your dreams will become reality, you'll finally be the person you hoped you would be with the life you hoped to have. But Q is not being unnecessarily negative. He's telling us the truth. He's being realistic about how limited things like self-help strategies and "if-you-only-believe" inspirational messages really are—or how long their positive impact really lasts.

In so many ways, life under the sun simply doesn't make sense. And being a Christian doesn't make this any less true. Being a Christian means that we can stop pretending this isn't true.[15]

Q's Search for Something Worthwhile

After Q has established the intrinsic problem with the world, he begins listing out all of the things he tried in his personal quest to find satisfaction and meaning in life.

> I said to myself, "Come on, let's try pleasure. Let's look for the 'good things' in life." But I found that this, too, was meaningless. So I said, "Laughter is silly. What good does it do to seek pleasure?" After much thought, I decided to cheer myself with wine. And while still seeking wisdom, I clutched at foolishness. In this way, I tried to experience the only happiness most people find during their brief life in this world.
>
> I also tried to find meaning by building huge homes for myself and by planting beautiful vineyards. I made gardens and parks, filling them with all kinds of fruit trees. I built reservoirs to collect the water to irrigate my many flourishing groves. I bought slaves, both men and women, and others were born into

my household. I also owned large herds and flocks, more than any of the kings who had lived in Jerusalem before me. I collected great sums of silver and gold, the treasure of many kings and provinces. I hired wonderful singers, both men and women, and had many beautiful concubines. I had everything a man could desire!

So I became greater than all who had lived in Jerusalem before me, and my wisdom never failed me. Anything I wanted, I would take. I denied myself no pleasure. I even found great pleasure in hard work, a reward for all my labors. But as I looked at everything I had worked so hard to accomplish, it was all so meaningless—like chasing the wind. There was nothing really worthwhile anywhere.

2:1-11

Q recounts his full-time, full-throttle search for meaning, for something that would dull the ache of life. He tried the very same things that so many of us try in a desperate attempt to find something to fill the empty place. If he were living in our era, perhaps his list would sound this way: "I tried to amuse myself and avoid anything serious. I tried using alcohol to numb myself. I bought the most house I could afford and had it landscaped by the best landscaper in town. Then I built a business empire complete with people to follow my orders and financial holdings to secure my future. I went to the concerts of my favorite bands and indulged in sex with as many partners as possible. I worked hard and played hard and never said no to myself. But none of it made me happy. At least not for very long."

We get it. However much money we have, we always want a little bit more. However much pleasure we experience, the satisfaction never lasts very long. Chasing after "enough" is always like chasing the wind. It's impossible to catch.

Q does seem to have come up with a helpful insight in the midst of his search. A little later in the book he says,

> Even so, I have noticed one thing, at least, that is good. It is good for people to eat, drink, and enjoy their work under the sun during the short life God has given them, and to accept their lot in life. And it is a good thing to receive wealth from God and the good health to enjoy it. To enjoy your work and accept your lot in life— this is indeed a gift from God.
>
> 5:18-19

Over the centuries some have taken his words and turned them into a hedonistic mantra about indulging ourselves while this life lasts since there is nothing after death. But that isn't really what Q is saying. He's telling us that in this world where there is so much that is *not* good, God has given us many good things. And he has given them to us for our enjoyment. In fact, it honors God when we enjoy these things in recognition that they are gifts from him, without turning them into things we demand from him.

So putting together Q's unsatisfying exploration of pleasure with his endorsement of simple pleasures, the takeaway seems to be this:

When we find ourselves unsatisfied in life, it's not that we don't have what we need to be happy; it's that we refuse to be happy with what we have.

Q wants us to enjoy today's meal even though we'll be hungry again tomorrow. He wants us to enjoy the accomplishment of today's work, even though someone else may profit from it. He wants us to enjoy the measure of health we've been given today even though the day is coming when death will overtake us. He seems to be saying to us, "Open your hands and receive what God is giving to you, even though it might not be everything you long for." Thankfulness for the things that money can buy, the honest work that earned the money, and the good health to enjoy them generates genuine happiness in the midst of this "unhappy business" (1:13, ESV) of life under the sun.

Q seems to want us to loosen our grip on "life as we dreamed it would be" so that we can take hold of "life as it is" and really enjoy it. He wants us to enjoy a delicious meal, a funny joke, a job well done, and the company of a good friend. He wants us to enjoy God's presence with us in the mundane, the ordinary, even the uncomfortable. He wants us to stop chasing the wind thinking that we will finally be happy when we get married, or get a promotion, or retire, or have children, or get our children raised. He wants us to learn to savor the simple pleasures of the life we have now.

Q's Invitation to Think about Death

As we enjoy the simple pleasures of this life, Q wants us to be fully cognizant that this life will likely be far shorter than we might think. He wants us, in a sense, to put on a particular set of glasses that will enable us to see this life more clearly. He wants us to look at life through the lens of death.

Now we're thinking that Q has gone from being negative to being morbid. But he's not being morbid; he's being wise. He's nudging us out of our comfortable denial of death, not to depress us but to impress upon us how facing our own mortality will actually add to our lives rather than take from them. Q tells us,

> The day you die is better than the day you are born.
> Better to spend your time at funerals than at parties.
> After all, everyone dies—
>> so the living should take this to heart. . . .
> A wise person thinks a lot about death,
>> while a fool thinks only about having a good
>>> time.
>
> 7:1-2, 4

He's saying to us:

Looking squarely into the reality of death doesn't ruin our lives; it informs our lives.

A few years ago I put together a book that included a number of short pieces about death written by ancient as well as modern writers. It's called *O Love That Will Not Let Me Go: Facing Death with Courageous Confidence in God.*[16] I think that if Q were around today, he would appreciate my effort to get people thinking about death.

But in working on the project, I discovered that people really don't want to think about death unless they're forced to. As I told people about my project, I noticed that they often recoiled. The idea of a whole book about death seemed morbid or depressing. I think some people responded that way because of a bit of superstition—a sense that they didn't want to read or think about death because then maybe they would die.

I hated to break it to them—but one day they *will* die. Refusing to think about or prepare for death has zero power to delay or avoid it. But soberly considering the reality of death does have power to add to our lives.

Does that sound crazy to you, or does it make sense?

I suppose if we're only focused on the process and potential pain of dying, our reluctance to consider death makes some sense. Certainly we don't like to think about the pain of separation from those we love that comes with death. But thinking and talking about death instead of denying and avoiding it is not morbid or depressing. It's liberating. It's freeing. It keeps us from being superficial. It helps us to focus on what matters and let go of what doesn't. It's at the heart of what it means to be wise, since wisdom refuses to ignore difficult realities.

For those who struggle with a sense of emptiness, soberly contemplating the reality of death reminds us that everything we acquire or achieve in this world has a limited shelf life. All of the things we think we simply must have to fill up the emptiness? Eventually we'll be forced to let go of them. The day will come when we will have to let go of everything, including life itself.

Perhaps we think that what we really need to be happy in life is to have a good marriage. Well, that commitment is simply "till death do us part." Human marriage will not last beyond this life. Even if we do find lasting love, one day we will let go of the one we love.

Or perhaps we believe that what we really need to fill the emptiness is a certain level of achievement or acclaim. Just when we think that being acknowledged for our achievement or accomplishment is what will fill us up, death elbows us in the ribs and reminds us that one day all of our trophies will be thrown in the trash, one day the building or business with our name on it will become rubble. Q says to us, "We all come to the end of our lives as naked and empty-handed as on the day we were born. We can't take our riches with us" (5:15).

Someday our children and grandchildren are going to go through all of the things we've accumulated that are in our attic, in a storage facility, or stashed away in drawers—things we didn't want to let go of yet left behind in death—and they're going to take most of it to the dump or to the secondhand store.

This reality not only prompts us to stop spending so much of our money and our lives collecting what we can't take with us, it also prompts us to want to invest ourselves and our money in the only things that will follow us out of this life.

Jesus said, "Don't store up treasures here on earth, where moths eat them and rust destroys them, and where thieves break in and steal. Store your treasures in heaven, where moths and rust cannot destroy, and thieves do not break in and steal" (Matthew 6:19-20). How do we lay up treasure in heaven? We use our money and possessions strategically and sacrificially to serve others in love and to advance God's Kingdom priority of his gospel being proclaimed to every tribe, tongue, and nation. And in the process, we discover that giving ourselves away like this doesn't empty out our lives; it fills them up with real meaning and lasting significance. Everything we do for Christ and through Christ and in Christ is going to matter into eternity.

> *Giving ourselves away . . . doesn't empty out our lives; it fills them up with real meaning and lasting significance. Everything we do for Christ and through Christ and in Christ is going to matter into eternity.*

Q's Limited Perspective

Our mentor has finished presenting Q's review of life under the sun, and in the final verses of the book of Ecclesiastes it's as if he turns toward us to tell us how we should think about all that Q has had to say about the meaninglessness of life.

Keep this in mind: The Teacher was considered wise, and he taught the people everything he knew. He listened carefully to many proverbs, studying and classifying them. The Teacher sought to find just the right words to express truths clearly.

12:9-10

The narrator tells us that certainly Q has gotten some things right. He has been good at identifying life's superficiality and contradictions. Evidently, however, he hasn't told us everything we need to know.

But, my child, let me give you some further advice: Be careful, for writing books is endless, and much study wears you out.

12:12

Our mentor seems to be warning us against spending a lifetime trying to make sense of this world, forever on a spiritual search without ever finding, deciding on, or embracing the truth. Perhaps he is saying to us, *You can search throughout your whole life, using your limited capacity and this world's limited understanding, and yet never become completely clear on how this world works and why God is working out his purposes in it the way that he is. So don't spend your life on an endless search thinking that if you can make sense of it all, then you will finally be satisfied. Put your trust in the God who may not have revealed everything to us that we would like to know, but who has revealed enough about himself to earn our trust.*

Put your trust in the God who may not have revealed everything to us that we would like to know, but who has revealed enough about himself to earn our trust.

Then he states his conclusion concerning what we should do with all that Q has told us. It is shorter and simpler than we might expect—perhaps even shorter and simpler than we might like:

> Here now is my final conclusion: Fear God and obey his commands, for this is everyone's duty.
>
> 12:13

Our mentor's response to Q's assertion that life is meaningless and nothing lasts is to give us a glimpse of what does, in fact, fill our lives with meaning and will matter forever: to live in this broken world with God at the center of our attention and as the object of our affections.

To fear God is to take God seriously, to acknowledge

him in our lives as the highest good, to revere him, to honor and worship him, and to center our lives on him. It is to live in a world that doesn't work right, trusting that while we can't make sense of everything, God can. While we can't see how everything will fit together for our good and for his glory, God can.

The last word our mentor leaves with us before we go our separate ways is this:

> God will judge us for everything we do,
> including every secret thing, whether good
> or bad.
>
> 12:14

How's that for a last word? Perhaps it sounds to you like one last blow of bitter reality. Perhaps you envision a long-bearded man in the town square wearing a signboard that says, "Prepare for judgment!" and pointing in your direction, rather than someone who cares about you and is sitting across from you in a coffee shop.

But perhaps these final words are actually intended to provide great encouragement. Our mentor seems to be assuring us that life actually isn't meaningless, as Q has repeatedly asserted. Our lives aren't simply a vapor that is going to disappear. Perhaps he is leaving us with this:

When life appears to have no meaning, it's not that our conclusion is wrong; it's that our perspective is limited.

Q has reviewed his experience of life from his vantage point of "under the sun." He has spoken from his own observation and reflection. But what seems to be missing is revelation—a word from God. So here at the end of the book, our mentor steps in to add to what Q has said. He wants us to know that while our limited perspective on life might suggest that how we live doesn't really matter and that death brings everything to an end, that isn't exactly true. In actuality, the day is going to come when we will see clearly that our lives have a God-saturated, God-oriented, God-directed purpose and meaning that lasts beyond our lifetimes. We have an enduring relationship with the one who created us, and the day is going to come when he will judge rightly—or, in other words, he will set things right in this world.

The day is going to come when we will see clearly that our lives have a God-saturated, God-oriented, God-directed purpose and meaning that lasts beyond our lifetimes.

As we sit and sip our coffee, considering what our mentor has said, we realize that we need his perspective on Q's review. But actually, we need even more than that because even our wise mentor has a limited perspective. While his words reflect all that Old Testament wisdom has to offer, they lack the full revelation you and I glean from the New Testament, the revelation of the mystery once hidden but now revealed in the person and work of Christ.

We have the fuller revelation of God himself, who, in the person of Jesus, entered into this life under the sun—into all of its brokenness, crookedness, coldness, and cruelty. Jesus experienced the frustration of this life as well as its simple pleasures. Most significantly, Jesus experienced death. But his death was not an ordinary death; it was a death-defeating death. His resurrection from death pierces through the pessimism and fatalism of Q's assessment of this world and infuses it with hope.

> *Because of the death and resurrection of Jesus and what they accomplished, we know that the frustration and futility of life in this world will not last forever.*

Because of the death and resurrection of Jesus and what they accomplished, we know that the frustration and futility of life in this world will not last forever. We know that "what we suffer now is nothing compared to the glory he will reveal to us later. . . . For we know that all creation has been groaning as in the pains of childbirth right up to the present time. And we believers also groan, even though we have the Holy Spirit within us as a foretaste of future glory" (Romans 8:18, 22-23).

Future glory. The Bible speaks about glory as something that is weighty. It tells us that "our present troubles are small and won't last very long. Yet they produce for us a glory that vastly outweighs them and will last forever!" (2 Corinthians 4:17). Here we have the antidote to meaninglessness, the opposite of having lives that are like a vanishing breath. If we are in Christ, we can be sure that far from simply fading away in death, our future will be weighted with a glory that will last forever.

In Christ, our lives will not prove to be like a vanishing breath. Instead, they will produce eternal glory. It won't be a glory we've created for ourselves, but rather a glory that has been shared with us, a glory that is even now transforming us. The reason we can anticipate sharing in this glory is not that we have feared God completely or obeyed his commands perfectly. Rather, we anticipate sharing in this glory because we are joined to Jesus. He is the one who feared God completely and obeyed his commands perfectly.

When we're joined to Christ, there is a weightiness to our lives that Q couldn't see from his perspective under the sun. Our coffee companion had a better sense of it, understanding that our fear of God and obedience to God matter beyond this life because of our ultimate accountability to God and our eternal relationship with him. But even he could not see as clearly as we can the weighty glory that is transforming our lives now and will define our lives in the new heaven and new earth.

The day is coming when our lives will not be lived under the sun. They will not be lived under the cloud of death in a world where what is wrong cannot be made right. Rather, we will live in a place that "has no need of sun or moon, for the glory of God illuminates" it (Revelation 21:23). "There will be no more death or sorrow or crying or pain. All these things are gone forever" (Revelation 21:4). The tension between what this world was created to be and how we experience it now will have finally been resolved.

Until that day, rather than allowing our perspective on this life—the seeming meaninglessness of it, the aching emptiness of it—to be shaped only by what we feel and what we can see, we allow it to be shaped by what God has revealed and what he has promised. And day by day, year by year, we find ourselves increasingly "strong and immovable. Always work[ing] enthusiastically for the Lord, [knowing] that nothing [we] do for the Lord is ever useless" (1 Corinthians 15:58). Even as we face the realities of this world that tempt us to see our lives as meaningless, we remind ourselves that Christ is, even now, filling our lives with meaning as the Spirit works to make us "more and more like him as we are changed into his glorious image" (2 Corinthians 3:18).

CHAPTER SEVEN

A TREMBLING TRUST

God Fills Our Emptiness with Faith

IN THE CLASSIC MOVIE *The Sound of Music*, young governess Maria has a way of dealing with difficult realities: She sings. One night, as the children she cares for begin to gather in her bed because of the brewing storm outside, she teaches them to sing about their favorite things as a way of distracting themselves from their fears.

I suppose distraction is one way to deal with difficult realities. Maybe that works with a dog bite, or a bee sting, or a bout of feeling sad. But what about when what has made us afraid is the possibility of losing our house after falling behind on the payments, or waiting to hear the diagnosis from the doctor, or anticipating a guilty verdict against our child who is facing legal charges? Will simply singing about our favorite things help us to not feel so bad when we're facing an empty bank account, an empty bed, or an empty future?

And if singing about our favorite things won't assuage our gripping fears, is there anything that will?

In the little Old Testament book of Habakkuk, we find the writings of a prophet who was gripped by frustration, confusion, and fear as he faced the future. And it wasn't because he hadn't heard from God. What stoked his fears was what God had clearly revealed to him.

From Habakkuk's perspective, he was living in a world devoid of justice, where the violence and other wickedness among God's people in Judah continued on unabated and unpunished. He simply could not understand why God had not done something about it. So he cried out to God, asking how long it was going to take for God to act.

And then God told him what he was going to do—but Habakkuk could make no sense of it. God told him that in response to the sin among his people, he was raising up the Babylonians, a nation notorious for its wickedness and cruelty, to march through Judah and destroy it. Habakkuk thought that surely he must not have heard God correctly. How could the God he had loved and served, a God who was pure and could not stand the sight of evil, actually use a nation that was even more wicked than Judah to deal with Judah's sins?

This just didn't seem right to Habakkuk. And we get that, don't we? Don't we wonder, at times, how God could allow a person, an organization, or a government that we see as not just compromised but outright evil to act in a way that takes away our home, our health, or our reputation?

The plans God revealed made no sense to Habakkuk, so he asked if God was going to let Babylon get away with its evil forever. And then he waited for God to explain himself.

God spoke to Habakkuk again, telling him to write down his words. He said, "This vision is for a future time. It describes the end, and it will be fulfilled" (Habakkuk 2:3).

Evidently, what God was about to explain to Habakkuk was not just for him and for the people of his day. God was about to explain how he works to bring about his intended purposes—and to explain it in such a way that generations to come would need to hear and understand. In fact, what Habakkuk wrote down on his tablet is what you and I need to hear and understand—especially when it seems as if God is not at work in our world, when it seems that there is no justice, or when what God is doing makes no sense to us and doesn't line up with what we think a good God would do.

God explained to Habakkuk that while he intended to use the Babylonians to be his instrument of judgment on unrepentant Judah, the Babylonians were not going to get a pass on their own wickedness forever. In fact, their day was coming; they would get what they deserved. They would be taken captive, plundered, shamed. Their wealth would turn to ashes. Babylon may have been sweeping throughout the known world in Habakkuk's day, filling it with cruelty, violence, and oppression. But one day, God told Habakkuk, when Babylon and all of its iterations over the centuries to come were no more, the world would be filled with something very different. "The earth will be filled with the knowledge of the glory of the LORD as the waters cover the sea" (Habakkuk 2:14, ESV). This is where human history is headed, God told Habakkuk. This will be the final result when all is said and done.

Habakkuk could hardly imagine that this could be true. He simply couldn't see that far into the future, that far beyond his present painful reality. So God told him what it was going to take to live in the present as he awaited this promised future, saying, "The righteous shall live by his faith" (Habakkuk 2:4, ESV). Habakkuk was going to need to live not by what he could see with his eyes in his day, but rather by placing all of his confidence in what God had said about a day to come in the future, a day when all will be made right.

Just as Habakkuk had to think this through, you and I have to think through what it is going to mean for us to live by faith in what God has said rather than by what we can see in our circumstances. Habakkuk knew that if the Babylonians were coming, devastation was about to sweep, not only through the nation that he loved, but also through his own life, through his own property and livelihood, through his own family. In the coming devastation, Habakkuk was likely to lose everything and be left with nothing.

So what did Habakkuk do after he thought it through? He sang. Habakkuk sang a song that was then written down so that the people in his day, the people facing devastation in the centuries to come, and people like you and me in our day could sing it too. Habakkuk's song is a demonstration of what it looks like to live by faith. It's a celebration of just judgment, an admission of real fear, a determination to have rugged joy, and an expectation of ultimate security. And we're invited to sing along.

You say you don't know the tune? Habakkuk tells us in the first verse that it's "according to shigionoth." Now I don't know that melody, but my guess is that it started off sounding a bit like a haunting Gregorian chant, as Habakkuk began his prayer song by singing:

> I have heard all about you, LORD.
>   I am filled with awe by your amazing works.
> In this time of our deep need,
>   help us again as you did in years gone by.
> And in your anger,
>   remember your mercy.

HABAKKUK 3:2

Habakkuk recognized that what God had done in the past served as the most reliable evidence of what he would do in the future. And a shift took place in Habakkuk's soul. Rather than continuing to argue with God, he welcomed God to work. But he did have a request: "In your anger, remember your mercy." He was saying, *God, in all of this upheaval and destruction, show mercy to the people on whom you've set your love. In the tumult of what is about to unfold, even though we rightly deserve to be caught up in the catastrophe, save us from complete annihilation.*

Then the tune changed a bit, perhaps beginning to sound a bit more like a triumphant battle hymn as Habakkuk started to recount God's victories against the enemies of his people in the past.

A Celebration of Just Judgment

Throughout the history of God's interaction with his people, God had repeatedly saved them—not *from* judgment but *through* judgment. He saved Adam and Eve through the judgment that came down in Eden. He saved Noah and his family through the judgment that rained down on the whole earth. He saved the nation of Israel through the judgment that came down in the plague of the death of the firstborn on the first Passover. And it is here in Israel's story that Habakkuk seemed to focus. He remembered how God had repeatedly saved his people through the judgment that descended on those who wanted to harm them on their way out of Egypt and to the Promised Land—on Pharaoh, on the Egyptians, and on the nations that attacked them as they traveled toward Canaan. Habakkuk remembered:

> *Throughout the history of God's interaction with his people, God had repeatedly saved them—not from judgment but through judgment.*

You marched across the land in anger
    and trampled the nations in your fury.
You went out to rescue your chosen people,
    to save your anointed ones.

HABAKKUK 3:12-13

As Habakkuk remembered that God, in his wrath, had extended mercy to his covenant people over and over again, that he had rescued them again and again, it strengthened his faith that God could not only be trusted to justly judge those who rightly deserve his anger; he could be trusted to rescue his own through that judgment.

As Habakkuk surveyed God's just judgment throughout the history of his people, Habakkuk began to genuinely believe that he could trust God to do right. God would do right by Babylon. He would do right by Judah. He would do right by Habakkuk.

But that newfound trust didn't take away Habakkuk's fear over what was about to happen. And I appreciate the humanness of the prophet here. He was appropriately afraid of the awesome power of God coming in judgment. He was understandably afraid of the disaster that was going to become a reality for all of his friends and neighbors and family. So his tune adjusted from a triumphant battle hymn to a softer, more melancholy song, admitting his very real fear.

An Admission of Real Fear

For Habakkuk, there would be a lot of misery in between the day of this revelation and the future salvation he was singing about. Evidently, having eyes of faith regarding a future salvation didn't take away all of his fear about what would happen in the in-between time.

> I trembled inside when I heard this;
>   my lips quivered with fear.
> My legs gave way beneath me,
>   and I shook in terror.
> I will wait quietly for the coming day
>   when disaster will strike the people
>   who invade us.

HABAKKUK 3:16

Habakkuk was trembling with fear, but he was determined to trust. He seemed to be saying, *I'm scared. I know there is heartache and loss ahead for me and for people I love, and there is a part of me that is terrified as I think about the Babylonian invaders showing up on our doorstep. But I refuse to let this fear grip and control me. I refuse to allow this difficulty in my short-term future rob me of my long-term hope. Because I believe that God will prove true on his promises to save his people, I can wait quietly. God has given me a glimpse of the day when the earth will be filled with the knowledge of the glory of the Lord as the waters cover the sea. And what I know to be true about my future glory is changing how I feel about, and how I intend to face, my present pain.*[17]

Habakkuk is giving us an honest song to sing as we seek to live by faith, and at this point the feel of the song changes once again. It moves from a confession of very real fear to a resolve to be joyful, even when the worst happens.

A Determination to Have Rugged Joy

> Even though the fig trees have no blossoms,
>   and there are no grapes on the vines;
> even though the olive crop fails,
>   and the fields lie empty and barren;
> even though the flocks die in the fields,
>   and the cattle barns are empty,
> yet I will rejoice in the LORD!
>   I will be joyful in the God of my
>   salvation!
>
> HABAKKUK 3:17-18

Since Habakkuk lived in an agrarian society, the fig tree not blossoming, the olive crop failing, and the cattle dying off represented a total loss of livelihood and way of life. He was facing empty fields and empty barns. Clearly faith for Habakkuk was not the modern-day version of "faith" that is often defined as believing that God is going to do a miracle to take all of the hard stuff away, that there will be a last-minute reprieve from the anticipated disaster. Habakkuk is showing us that real faith is being determined to have genuine joy even as we face devastating loss in life. It's the kind of genuine faith in the face of disaster that we see again and again in the Bible. Habakkuk's rugged trust reminds us of Job, who said this in the midst of devastation:

> *Habakkuk is showing us that real faith is being determined to have genuine joy even as we face devastating loss in life.*

> As for me, I know that my Redeemer lives,
> and he will stand upon the earth at last.
> And after my body has decayed,
> yet in my body I will see God!
>
> JOB 19:25-26

It reminds us of David's determination not to fear in the face of death:

> Even when I walk
> through the darkest valley,
> I will not be afraid,
> for you are close beside me.

Your rod and your staff
    protect and comfort me.
PSALM 23:4

It reminds us of Shadrach, Meshach, and Abednego, who said to the king of Babylon as he made the fire hotter,

If we are thrown into the blazing furnace, the God whom we serve is able to save us. He will rescue us from your power, Your Majesty. But even if he doesn't, we want to make it clear to you, Your Majesty, that we will never serve your gods or worship the gold statue you have set up.
DANIEL 3:17-18

Habakkuk's confidence in the glory to come after suffering reminds us of Paul's confidence in what was to come after his earthly suffering came to an end:

That is why we never give up. Though our bodies are dying, our spirits are being renewed every day. For our present troubles are small and won't last very long. Yet they produce for us a glory that vastly outweighs them and will last forever!
2 CORINTHIANS 4:16-17

In spite of fear we can wait, confident that we have nothing to ultimately fear. In spite of loss we can rejoice, confident that all we truly need is ours in Christ. One day everywhere we look we will see the glory of God. This is what it looks like and sounds like to live by faith and not by sight.

Habakkuk was confident that God was in control of the details and even the disasters in his life. He knew where the story of his life and this world is headed— toward a time and place in which all evil will be overthrown and all will be made right.

> *One day everywhere we look we will see the glory of God. This is what it looks like and sounds like to live by faith and not by sight.*

An Expectation of Ultimate Security

As Habakkuk brought his song to a close, though he maintained his realism about the threats on his horizon, he sang about something far more real to him.

> The Sovereign LORD is my strength!
> He makes me as surefooted as a deer,
>   able to tread upon the heights.

HABAKKUK 3:19

Habakkuk was confident that the Lord would enable him to navigate the difficult situations that were ahead for him. He would be "surefooted" like a mountain deer that is able to safely navigate rugged terrain and dangerous drop-offs. He was choosing to live by faith—not the kind of faith that believed God was going to miraculously show up and shield him *from* harm, but faith that God would preserve him *through* harm.

I want that kind of faith. Don't you? But how does that happen? Is this kind of faith in the face of disaster only for certain personality types? Is it only for the super spiritual among us? Is this one of those "fake it till you make it" things?

A Filling with Faith

Pastor Rico Tice says that "faith is the ability to live in light of unexperienced events"[18]—those in the past as well as in the future. By gazing intently into the Scriptures, we consider carefully how God has acted in the past, and we also savor the promises he has made regarding the future. Living by faith is thinking, feeling, and acting on those things rather than solely on what we are seeing, experiencing, or feeling in the present.

This means that if we're going to live by faith, we need to invest ourselves in knowing what God has done in the past and has promised for the future. And I don't mean that our focus is primarily on what God has done in our own lives in the past. What stirs up this kind of confidence in God is our ongoing exposure to what he has done over history in relationship to his people. It is reading, hearing, and considering deeply what God has done and what he has promised in the Bible that generates this kind of faith. As we saturate ourselves in God's Word, we understand more clearly what God has promised and what he has not promised. And we become increasingly willing to risk everything on God's promises being fully reliable.

> *By gazing intently into the Scriptures, we consider carefully how God has acted in the past, and we also savor the promises he has made regarding the future.*

Faith is believing in what you can't see. But that's not the same thing as blind faith. "Faith looks at observable realities, yet looks beyond them to take into account what is invisible—the power of God"[19] and his solid commitment to bring about his purposes and plans in his world. When Habakkuk looked around at his present reality, he could not see that God was doing anything at all. But he looked back at what God had done in the past for his people, and he considered what God had promised to do in the future, and on that basis he chose to trust God in the present.

Maybe you're thinking to yourself, *I'd like to have that kind of faith, but I just don't.* This is not something a person can work up in herself. God is the one who fills us with this kind of faith as we are made alive spiritually by the Holy Spirit and joined to Christ. You see, Jesus is the only person who ever perfectly lived by faith. That's why the writer of the book of Hebrews tells us that we live by faith "by keeping our eyes on Jesus, the champion who initiates and perfects our faith" (Hebrews 12:2). If we have become joined to Jesus by faith, we actually have everything we need to live this way.

My friend, we don't want to live in this world based on what we can see. If we look at our lives more deeply than merely considering our current circumstances, if we are willing to look into the reality of our own souls, sight will tell us that we have sinned and fallen short of the glory of God, that we rightly deserve nothing less than utter destruction. But faith sees something else. Faith perceives and believes that on the cross, Christ experienced the utter destruction we deserve so that we can anticipate experiencing the abundant blessing that he deserves. Faith looks at the past saving works of God in the Passover, at the Red Sea, and most significantly at the Cross and Resurrection, and trusts that God's saving work is not simply a thing of the past. It trusts that we are, even now, being saved from the sin that would destroy us and that we will one day be delivered safely into the presence of God.

Faith enables us to sing a song like one I grew up singing, a hymn that set the words of 2 Timothy 1:12 (KJV) to music: "For I know whom I have believed, and am persuaded that he is able to keep that which I've committed unto him against that day." Though it is less singable, I like how the NLT translates the same verse: "I know the one in whom I trust, and I am sure that he is able to guard what I have entrusted to him until the day of his return." Paul seems to be suggesting in these words that we can't necessarily expect that God is going to provide us everything right now that he has promised to us, but rather, we are persuaded that he will deliver on all of his promises on "that day." What day is that? It's the final day of salvation through judgment. The day of his return.

In Revelation 18 we read again about the city of Babylon. Pastor Colin Smith says, "Babylon is the generic term for all of the rising and falling powers of the world in arrogance and defiance of God."[20] At the end of the Bible, indeed at the end of human history as we know it, we find the ultimate fulfillment of what God promised to Habakkuk when he assured him that Babylon would get her due. We read:

O Babylon, you great city!
In a single moment
   God's judgment came on you. . . .
Rejoice over her fate, O heaven
   and people of God and apostles and prophets!
For at last God has judged her
   for your sakes.

REVELATION 18:10, 20

On that day, judgment will come down. But all who are joined to Christ by faith will be saved through that judgment.

God has a timetable, and God's timetable will be adhered to. The end will come. In the meantime it might seem as if God has forgotten what he promised. It might seem as if nothing is ever going to change, that wrongs will never be righted, that God is taking a really long time to set things right in this world. But like Habakkuk, we have to be willing to wait. We have to wait through the devastation, wait through the fear, wait for God to bring the story he is writing in his world to its appointed end, which will really be a new beginning.

And while we wait, we sing. We don't simply distract ourselves from our difficulties as we wait by singing about doorbells and sleigh bells or schnitzel with noodles. We sing to stir up the faith that God has given to us by joining us to Christ. Perhaps we take Habakkuk's song and adjust it to the difficulties in our own lives, creating a song that goes something like this:

Even if my income dries up
And my savings are gone,
Even if I face a devastating diagnosis
And lose my dignity in the process,

Even if my integrity is questioned
And my reputation ruined;
Yet I will choose daily to be happy in Christ.
I will smile at the future because I am protected and
provided for in Christ.

None of these things is the source of my strength or
security; God alone is my strength.
Christ in me enables me to navigate dangerous and
difficult circumstances.
Because of Christ, I know that my future is full
of glory.

My friend, your confidence is not that God is going to fix everything for you in the here and now. Your confidence is that though there may be significant losses in this life, huge places of emptiness, there is divine full-ness in your future. One day his glory is going to fill this earth like the waters cover the sea. Faith will become sight. And when it does, we won't be able to keep from singing. We'll sing our favorite song about our favorite person: "Great and marvelous are your works, O Lord God, the Almighty. Just and true are your ways . . . for your righteous deeds have been revealed" (Revelation 15:3-4).

CHAPTER EIGHT

A HIDDEN TREASURE

God Fills Our Emptiness with Joy

DAVID AND I occasionally catch an episode of *Antiques Roadshow* on PBS. On this television show, ordinary people bring in objects of art, furnishings, collectibles, and other things that they've had stashed in the attic or around the house, family heirlooms that have been handed down through generations, hoping that the experts on the show can give them a sense of what these items are worth. And, of course, they're hoping to find out that their items are worth even more than they might have expected.

If you've ever watched the show, then you know it is not an altogether unlikely scenario that an object someone has had around the house or bought at a garage sale for a hundred dollars might end up being worth thousands. It's happened many times on the show. For example, in 2012 a man in Corpus Christi, Texas, brought in a painting that for years had been hanging behind a door in his family's home. Dated to 1904, the "El Albañil" oil painting by Diego Rivera was authenticated and appraised to be worth between eight hundred thousand and one million dollars. All those years on the back side of a door, no one knowing its true value.

In 2014, a woman whose great-great-grandmother had run a boarding house in which the Boston baseball team stayed during their first season in 1871 brought in some sports memorabilia passed down to her. Her Boston Red Stockings baseball cards and a letter from the first lineup were appraised at one million dollars.[21] Who would have guessed, in 1871, that the baseball cards from a start-up team would end up being so valuable? Think of all of the baseball cards from 1871 that were discarded along the way, assumed to be worthless.

The key to *Antiques Roadshow* is the experts who know how to rightly evaluate the worth of the objects brought in for appraisal. Of course, this skill of knowing how to rightly evaluate the worth of things is not only important on *Antiques Roadshow*. It's important in life—in your life and mine. You and I often don't know how to properly value things. And because of this, we sometimes hold on to what we think is valuable, when it really has little lasting value. Likewise, we refuse to take hold of what is supremely valuable. The stories we will consider in this chapter are meant to train us in this skill of rightly valuing and making wise trades so that we will not end up empty-handed.

Up to this point in this book, most of the stories and sections of the Bible we've looked at have been about people whose emptiness was the result of something that was taken or withheld from them, something that was lost because of circumstances beyond their control. But this chapter is a bit different. The people we'll meet here had a choice about whether or not they would be empty, whether or not they would divest themselves of the things that mattered most to them so that they could enrich themselves with something—or someone—far more valuable. Their stories call us to consider yet another way that God can do—and in fact does—his best work with empty in our lives. Sometimes he calls us to let go of what is worth less so that we can take hold of what is of inestimable worth.

Sadly Unwilling to Give All

Three of the Gospels tell the same story of a young man who appeared to have everything and who came to Jesus (see Matthew 19:16-30; Mark 10:17-31; and Luke 18:18-30). By looking at all three passages we learn a few details about him: He was rich, and he was a religious leader. He had plenty of resources to finance a comfortable lifestyle, plenty of morality and religiosity to engender the respect of others, and plenty of authority to get his way in the world. But there was one thing he wasn't sure about, one thing he wanted to make sure he possessed.

> Someone came to Jesus with this question: "Teacher, what good deed must I do to have eternal life?"
>
> MATTHEW 19:16

It's a good question, an important question. Clearly this young man was thinking long-term rather than merely short-term. He was a step ahead of most people in the world who are too preoccupied with concerns of this life to give much thought to the next. This man was thinking more deeply.

His question does, however, reveal an assumption: that what he sought could be apprehended by something he could do, that eternal life was available to him through a "good deed" that he could complete. Evidently he had done plenty of what he deemed "good deeds" in his short life, and he just wanted to make sure that he had checked off all of the right boxes on the list.

So far in his life he had been able to do everything he'd set his mind to do, and he was quite sure he could ring this bell too. But Jesus pulled the rug out from underneath his assumption.

> "Why ask me about what is good?" Jesus replied. "There is only One who is good. But to answer your question—if you want to receive eternal life, keep the commandments."
>
> MATTHEW 19:17

Seemingly the young man just ignored this suggestion that his goodness was really not that good compared to God. He heard Jesus say, "Keep the commandments." Yes, he could do that. He'd always done that, hadn't he? He was feeling good about his chances of getting what he came for, but maybe he thought he should get Jesus to be a bit more specific.

> "Which ones?" the man asked.
> And Jesus replied: "'You must not murder. You must not commit adultery. You must not steal. You must not testify falsely. Honor your father and mother. Love your neighbor as yourself.'"
>
> MATTHEW 19:18-19

Notice that Jesus did not list out all ten of the Ten Commandments. He listed five of the ten, and his last sentence was the summary of those five. He left out the first tablet of the law—the commandments about loving God alone, not having idols, not taking God's name in vain, and keeping his day as holy. Jesus also left off the final commandment, "You must not covet." Can these be accidental omissions? Of course not.

> "I've obeyed all these commandments," the
> young man replied. "What else must I do?"
> MATTHEW 19:20

At this point in Mark's telling of this story, he inserts something not found in the other Gospel accounts. Mark writes, "Looking at the man, Jesus felt genuine love for him" (Mark 10:21). Mark wants us to know that what Jesus was about to ask of the man flowed out of compassion for him. Jesus loved this young man too much to allow him to go on assuming that eternal life was something he could acquire through his own effort. Jesus loved him too much to allow him to be ignorant of the true condition of his heart toward God. He knew where this man's pressure point was, what he loved the most, so he went right for it.

Jesus told him, "If you want to be perfect, go
and sell all your possessions and give the money
to the poor, and you will have treasure in
heaven. Then come, follow me."

MATTHEW 19:21

There they are, the missing commandments from
the earlier list. Jesus knew what was missing in this
man's heart—love for God—and what his heart was
full of—the love of money. Money was the god he put
before the one true God. It was the idol he worshiped.
His lack of real love for God meant that in his role as a
religious leader he was taking the Lord's name in vain.
And while he might have been diligent at keeping the
Sabbath according to the laws of the Pharisees, his mind
and his heart were set on his money seven days a week.

Jesus then called the man to obey the final commandment, to not covet what others have, by doing the
opposite: giving away what he loved to others.

Of course the sticking point in what Jesus was telling
him to do was that little word *all*. Jesus told him to sell
"all" of his possessions.

"All?" we want to say along with this man.

The young man was so stuck on that word that
perhaps he missed what was being promised to him
in return: "treasure in heaven." Perhaps he thought

this sounded too other-worldly to have any real value. Perhaps because he couldn't imagine it, he simply couldn't believe that it would not only have more value than the treasure he had now but also bring him more pleasure, more comfort, and more security.

He had come to Jesus because he was aware of an empty place in his well-ordered life—an empty place where "eternal security" or "confidence of full acceptance before God" was meant to be. And he was hoping that he could just do what was necessary to add this piece, as he had already added so many other things to his life. But instead of telling him how to add something, Jesus called him to let go of everything. Jesus asked this rich man to give away his riches. He asked this powerful man to surrender control of his day-to-day life.

Perhaps the young man took some time to think it through, to weigh his options. He rather enjoyed his money and everything that came with it. With money came power and prestige, and he probably liked the way people treated him, hoping to curry favor with him. He loved the pleasures that money could buy—eating at the nicest restaurants and going on the most extravagant vacations. Money gave him freedom he enjoyed, enabling him to do what he wanted to do as well as pay other people to do what he didn't want to do. He liked that he could afford the latest gadgets that made his life easier and the luxuries that made his life more comfortable. He didn't want to give any of that up.

And I get that; don't you? I'm all for loving Jesus and having eternal life and doing my best to obey his commands. But if I'm honest, I'd rather add the promise of "eternal life" to my collection of creature comforts. I don't want to have to surrender any of them.

Instead of telling this man what he needed to add to his life to secure his future, Jesus told him what he had to surrender to secure his future: Everything. And for this young man, it was just too much—too much to ask, too much to expect.

Instead of telling the rich young ruler what he needed to add to his life to secure his future, Jesus told him what he had to surrender to secure his future: Everything.

> At this the man's face fell, and he went away
> sad, for he had many possessions.
> MARK 10:22

Only moments before, he had approached Jesus with self-confident expectation. And now, he was walking away from Jesus in stunned sorrow. We usually call him the rich young ruler. But perhaps we should call him the sad young ruler who couldn't see how poor he really was and how rich Jesus wanted to make him.

As the young man evaluated the relative worth of his possessions and the treasure in heaven that Jesus was offering, he decided that following Jesus wasn't worth it.

And don't we make the same decision at times?

- Intimacy with Jesus isn't worth getting up a little earlier.
- Fellowship with Jesus' body and hearing his Word preached isn't worth missing the ball game.
- Sharing in the suffering of Jesus isn't worth putting our job or reputation at risk.
- Sharing the gospel of Jesus isn't worth going to the other side of the world, or the other side of town, or maybe even the other side of the street.
- Becoming holy like Jesus isn't worth saying no to watching certain shows or blocking certain websites.
- Serving Jesus isn't worth losing our freedom to use our time as we please.

Oh, how we need to reckon with the call of Jesus in our lives to value things rightly. How we need the worth of Jesus to loom large in our estimation so that it becomes unthinkable that we would walk away holding on to what will one day prove to be worthless, refusing to take hold of him.

The Gospel writers tell us that this man had many possessions. But really we can see that his many possessions had *him*. They had him in their grip. They had his heart in their vise.

Possessions and wealth are like that. For all of us. Yet when the Bible talks about "rich people" who will find it so hard to get into heaven, we're always wanting to point to those who are at least one rung higher on the economic ladder than we are. But if we look at our lives in context of the wider world, most of us who have the disposable income to buy this book and the discretionary time to read it will be forced to admit that we are, indeed, among the truly wealthy of the world.

Of course, when Jesus told his disciples immediately following this encounter that "it is easier for a camel to go through the eye of a needle than for a rich person to enter the Kingdom of God" (Matthew 19:24), he wasn't categorically condemning those with wealth. In fact, this is the only time in the Gospels that Jesus calls a rich person to give away all of his money. Jesus called this particular man to give away all of his wealth because it was a danger to his soul. Jesus sees wealth, and the self-reliance, self-indulgence, self-importance, and self-security that often come with it, as a potential stumbling block to entering into his Kingdom. Jesus knows that earthly riches often have the power to blind us to the value of heavenly riches. Earthly riches keep us from understanding the true value of things.

Because this sad, young ruler didn't understand the true value of things, imagine all he missed out on—the joy of being with Jesus, being taught by Jesus, being used by Jesus. What a tragedy to be large-and-in-charge but to miss out on rich relationship with Christ and a life lived under the authority of Christ.

Imagine the conflict in the young man's soul as he made the long walk home. But as sad as he was on that day as he walked away from Jesus, imagine the sadness he experienced on the day when he finally did have to give everything away, leave it all behind, as he entered not into eternal life but into eternal death with nothing. Nothing. Nothing but eternal sadness.

Joyfully Willing to Sell All

While three of the Gospel writers include this story of the rich young ruler who refused to give all and went away sad, only Matthew includes the two companion parables we want to look at next. These parables tell stories that are almost the opposite of the sad young ruler. In the middle of a series of seven parables that all have the same aim—to reveal something of the mystery of the Kingdom of Heaven—Jesus tells the very short stories of two people: a field laborer and a pearl merchant. One is at the top of the ladder of wealth and privilege, and the other is at the bottom. But they have something very important in common.

> The kingdom of heaven is like treasure hidden in a field, which a man found and covered up. Then in his joy he goes and sells all that he has and buys that field.
>   Again, the kingdom of heaven is like a merchant in search of fine pearls, who, on finding one pearl of great value, went and sold all that he had and bought it.
> MATTHEW 13:44-46, ESV

This story of a treasure hidden in a field is a bit foreign to us because these days we have banks or vaults to keep our money and valuables safe. In ancient days, however, it was completely normal for a wealthy person to take a treasure—coins, currency, or jewelry—and hide it or bury it for safekeeping until it was needed. But occasionally the person who buried it died or forgot where it was hidden. That is the scenario behind the parable Jesus told of treasure buried in a field.

When the owner of the field sent the worker out to prepare it for planting, he was unaware of the treasure hidden there. He saw only a field of dirt that needed a lot of work. And, of course, that's all the man working in the field saw too. But then as he turned the soil he hit something with his shovel, and when he examined what he had found, he realized that what he had unearthed was worth more than everything he owned and then some.

There would be a cost involved for the field laborer to make the treasure he had found his own. It would cost him everything. And as he stood in the field and ran the numbers in his head, he knew that he must do whatever was necessary, let go of whatever was necessary, in order to have the treasure. To have the treasure in the field, he had to have the field. So he sold what was worth less—everything he owned—to purchase what was worth more.

In this first parable we have a common laborer who wasn't particularly looking for treasure but stumbled upon it. In the second parable we have a wealthy merchant who spent all of his days in search of fine pearls. One day he was in the market and he spotted it—the pearl he had spent a lifetime searching for and thought he might never find. This pearl was worth more than the rest of his collection combined, more than all his pearl-trading business had provided for him and his family. There would be a high cost for the pearl merchant to have the choice pearl; it would cost him everything. But because the pearl was worth it, he went home and sold all his possessions so he could buy this one pearl. He sold what was worth less so he could purchase what was worth more.

There was undoubtedly a large differential between the actual amount of personal net worth that was sold off by the field laborer and what was sold off by the pearl merchant. But in another sense, the cost was the same. Both were willing to sell *all*, surrender *all*.

Imagine what it looked like as the field laborer, who had very little to begin with, began selling off everything he owned. His tools were the source of his livelihood, but he sold them. His mule was his only transportation, but he sold it. Everyone around him who had not yet seen the treasure could only see loss.

And imagine what it looked like for the pearl merchant to begin selling off his pearl collection. He'd traveled the world to add to it. Then he sold his big house and his fine clothes. People probably wondered, "How is he going to eat? You can't eat a pearl! Where is he going to live? You can't find shelter from the cold in a pearl!" Everyone who stood around as all of his holdings were auctioned off could only see his liquidation of

GOD DOES HIS BEST WORK WITH EMPTY

assets as loss. They couldn't see the gain—the gain that was worth all of the loss.

Of course Jesus is using these two parables to teach us. So what is the point he is trying to make?

The treasure that is worth selling everything else to have? Jesus.

The choice pearl worth selling everything else to have? Jesus.

> *Whatever must go, whatever must be abandoned to have Jesus—he's worth it. He's worth it now, and he will be worth it into eternity.*

Whatever must go, whatever must be abandoned to have him—he's worth it. He's worth it now, and he will be worth it into eternity. Oh, how we wish that sad young ruler had realized this. Oh, how we need to realize this ourselves! The more real this becomes to us, the more we recognize what Jesus is truly worth, the more joyful our relinquishment of whatever we must let go of to have him becomes.

Joyfully Anticipating Receiving All

You see, that's what catches our attention—the joy with which the field laborer paid the enormous cost. Jesus said, "*In his joy* he goes and sells all." Not joy after he had the treasure. Joy in the selling, joy in the emptying, joy in anticipation of having and enjoying the treasure from then on. There seems to be great joy in the very act of emptying out his assets in pursuit of the prize.

This story is telling us that Jesus is of such worth, such beauty, that there is incredible joy in letting go of whatever it takes to have him in your life. Eternal joy.

How could the laborer have joy as he let go of what had once been so valuable and meaningful to him? How could the pearl merchant have sold off so many beautiful things? Their joy was in anticipation of all they would gain.

And this, my friend, is how you and I can experience joy in letting go of whatever it is that we love and enjoy that is keeping us from allowing Jesus to take up full residence and authority in our lives. The way that we become people who have outrageous joy in spite of what it may cost us to identify with Jesus, speak up for Jesus, or serve Jesus is to anticipate all we have to gain.

Sometimes, on this side of eternity, all we can see is the cost. That's what was weighing heavily on the minds of the disciples as they watched the rich young religious leader walk away so sad.

Then Peter began to speak up. "We've given up everything to follow you," he said.

MARK 10:28

Sometimes we wonder if what we've given up to follow Jesus, the way we've been emptied because of our allegiance to him or our willingness to suffer for him, will really be worth it. So we need to lean in to listen to what Jesus said in response to Peter.

> "Yes," Jesus replied, "and I assure you that everyone who has given up house or brothers or sisters or mother or father or children or property, for my sake and for the Good News, will receive now in return a hundred times as many houses, brothers, sisters, mothers, children, and property—along with persecution. And in the world to come that person will have eternal life. But many who are the greatest now will be least important then, and those who seem least important now will be the greatest then."
>
> MARK 10:29-31

Jesus assures all who follow him that we will never regret anything we have surrendered for his sake. We can let it all go with joy, joy that is aroused through confidence in what will one day be ours.

To nurture this kind of joy in anticipation, we have to regularly remind ourselves of what we've been promised regarding what is to come. We have to relish what is ahead for us. We have to let what the Scriptures tell us about the treasure awaiting us fill us with anticipatory joy. So we read and think about and savor words like these:

> God blesses you when people mock you and persecute you and lie about you and say all sorts of evil things against you because you are my followers. Be happy about it! Be very glad! For a great reward awaits you in heaven.
>
> MATTHEW 5:11-12

Jesus assures all who follow him that we will never regret anything we have surrendered for his sake. We can let it all go with joy, joy that is aroused through confidence in what will one day be ours.

> Don't store up treasures here on earth, where moths eat them and rust destroys them, and where thieves break in and steal. Store your treasures in heaven, where moths and rust cannot destroy, and thieves do not break in and steal. Wherever your treasure is, there the desires of your heart will also be.
>
> MATTHEW 6:19-21

What we suffer now is nothing compared to the glory he will reveal to us later.

ROMANS 8:18

No eye has seen, no ear has heard,
    and no mind has imagined
what God has prepared
    for those who love him.

1 CORINTHIANS 2:9

And now the prize awaits me—the crown of righteousness, which the Lord, the righteous Judge, will give me on the day of his return. And the prize is not just for me but for all who eagerly look forward to his appearing.

2 TIMOTHY 4:8

When the Great Shepherd appears, you will receive a crown of never-ending glory and honor.

1 PETER 5:4

You love him even though you have never seen him. Though you do not see him now, you trust him; and you rejoice with a glorious, inexpressible joy. The reward for trusting him will be the salvation of your souls.

1 PETER 1:8-9

In his kindness God called you to share in his eternal glory by means of Christ Jesus. So after you have suffered a little while, he will restore, support, and strengthen you, and he will place you on a firm foundation.

1 PETER 5:10

How do we know that setting our hearts and minds on the treasure of what awaits us in heaven will enable us to let go of things in this life with joy? Because that is exactly what enabled Jesus to give all. Hebrews 12 tells us, "Because of the joy awaiting him, he endured the cross, disregarding its shame. Now he is seated in the place of honor beside God's throne" (12:2). Jesus gave all. Jesus paid the ultimate cost—the cost of his life—to have us as his treasured possession. Jesus was able to give all with joy because he anticipated what was awaiting him—redemption, resurrection, restoration, reunion, reward. And as we are joined to Jesus by faith, we find ourselves increasingly willing to relinquish what we have foolishly assumed will bring us joy in order to more fully enjoy him.

One day you and I are going to see with our eyes the treasure that has been hidden from the eyes of this world. One day we're going to enter into the presence of the one pearl of great value, Jesus Christ. We're going to experience in reality what we take hold of by faith now—that everything we have let go of in this life so we can take hold of Christ will have been worth it. Loss will have become gain.

Perhaps there are those you know and love who have gone before you. For them, faith has become sight. What do you think they would want to say to you about the wisdom of surrendering all to have Jesus? I suspect they might say something like this:

Don't listen to what this world tells you about what is valuable and what will make you happy!

They now see clearly what has value into eternity, what makes a person happy forever.

They might say:

With eyes of faith, see the beauty and value in the one pearl of great value, the person of Jesus Christ, and in joy, surrender anything and everything you must in order to have him. It might be a costly trade, but it will not prove to be a foolish trade. All of your loss will become gain.

In fact, this is the trade the apostle Paul was willing to make: "Whatever gain I had, I counted as loss for the sake of Christ. Indeed, I count everything as loss because of the surpassing worth of knowing Christ Jesus my Lord. For his sake I have suffered the loss of all things and count them as rubbish, in order that I may gain Christ" (Philippians 3:7-8, ESV).

While some of us would like to be able to say that we see the worth of Jesus so clearly that we've been willing to pay whatever cost is required to have him, what we invest our lives in reveals the truth about what we really value. We find ourselves in need of what Thomas Chalmers, a nineteenth-century preacher in Scotland, described in his sermon entitled "The Expulsive Power of a New Affection." Chalmers said, "The Gospel of Jesus Christ is expulsive in its power. It expels lesser treasures. It awakens a new appetite, a new affection, a new sense, a new taste, a new longing in the heart that nothing but Jesus can fill. That longing and that delight in Christ expels every rival."[22]

This is what Jesus says happens in the heart of the person who finds the treasure: The treasure captures her heart so that nothing else comes close to mattering in comparison. She relinquishes it all with joy. A new affection rules her heart and expels everything else her life used to revolve around. The good news of the gospel is that we can lose everything this world tells us has value—reputation, opportunity, wealth, power, attractiveness—and still have everything that will make us happy forever if we have him.

The day is going to come when we will be able to see that God indeed did his best work in our lives as he gave us the grace to empty ourselves of what was once so valuable, so important to us, and in the process, filled us with joy. Anticipatory joy now. Eternal joy in his presence.

> You make known to me the path
> of life;
>   in your presence there is
>   fullness of joy;
>   at your right hand are
>   pleasures forevermore.

PSALM 16:11, ESV

Forever pleasures replacing the fleeting pleasures of your life. Fullness of joy infused into the emptiness of your life.

CONCLUSION

A Prayer for Filling

OVER THE COURSE of the previous chapters we've gazed into profound emptiness experienced by the people of God—into the seemingly insatiable cravings of the Israelites in the wilderness, the bitter losses of Naomi, the cruel circumstances faced by Mephibosheth, the insatiable thirst of the woman at the well, the meaninglessness experienced by Qoheleth, the destruction anticipated by Habakkuk, and finally the trades made by the field worker and pearl merchant. And I'm hopeful that along the way, you've become convinced along with me that God really does do his best work with empty.

So now where does this leave us? I think it leads us to a place of prayer. Rather than simply presuming upon God to fill our emptiness, we need to pray, we need to plead with him to fill our emptiness in the way that only he can. Of course, if we set the agenda in our prayers, we will likely ask him to fill our emptiness the way we think is best. So perhaps we should instead allow the Scriptures to shape our prayers. The Bible shows us what to pray for and leads us into praying the kinds of prayers that our Father delights to answer.

Paul's Prayer for Filling

Before we go, let's consider a prayer Paul prayed, a prayer in which he asked that God would fill those he was praying for. His prayer can serve as a guide for us as we seek to talk to God about the emptiness in our lives. Here's Paul's prayer:

> For this reason I bow my knees before the
> Father, from whom every family in heaven
> and on earth is named, that according to the
> riches of his glory he may grant you to be
> strengthened with power through his Spirit
> in your inner being, so that Christ may dwell
> in your hearts through faith—that you, being
> rooted and grounded in love, may have strength
> to comprehend with all the saints what is the
> breadth and length and height and depth,
> and to know the love of Christ that surpasses
> knowledge, that you may be filled with all the
> fullness of God.
>
> EPHESIANS 3:14-19, ESV

In the first part of the prayer, Paul asks for power. Where does he pray this power would do its work? "In [our] inner being." Paul is praying for power that will go to work in our inner lives—our thought lives, our emotional lives. And why does he want us to have this power? "So that Christ may dwell in [our] hearts." He wants not just something but someone to move into the emptiness in our lives. He wants Christ to make his home in our hearts. He is praying that Christ would not simply take up residence in our lives but transform our hearts into homes that reflect his character, his preferences, his reality, his holiness, his fullness.

That's the first thing Paul prays for—that we will experience the power of God in the interior of our lives as Christ makes his home there, much as God made his home in the Most Holy Place of the Tabernacle. And then Paul continues with another request: He prays that we would have the power we need to comprehend, to truly grasp, the love that Christ has for us. He doesn't just want us to know *about* that love; he prays that we would experience it, that it would be real to us. I think he wants us to be a bit overwhelmed by it, certainly moved by it.

The people he's praying for already know that God loves them, so it's clear that Paul is praying for more than simple knowledge. He's praying that the magnitude, the expansiveness, the limitlessness, the sacrificial generosity of God's love for them would fill up the empty places inside them where loneliness lingers, where doubts simmer, where hopelessness hides. Paul wants them—and us—to feel and know the love of God in Christ for a particular purpose—so that we will be "filled to the measure of all the fullness of God" (Ephesians 3:19, NIV).

"The fullness of God" filling up our "inner being" is the ultimate answer to our emptiness.

God is holy. Paul is praying that the holiness of God would fill our lives, crowding out any lingering love for sin.

God is love. He's praying that the love of God will fill our lives so that we won't so quickly question it when hard things happen.

God is good. He's praying that God's goodness will so fill our lives that our instinctual response to bad news, bad people, and bad treatment will be goodness—God-like, God-energized goodness.

My Prayer for Filling

Along with Paul, I pray that you'll be strengthened in your inner being—strengthened with the power you need to welcome Christ to make himself at home there. As he does, I pray that you'll allow him to make the changes that are needed. And along with Paul, I pray that morning by morning, day by day, and night by night the love of God for you will loom large—larger than your fears, larger than your questions, larger than your disappointments.

I pray that God will do his best work with the emptiness in your life, just as he did in the lives of the children of Israel as they spent forty years in the wilderness, threatened by the kind of cravings that would tempt them to return to slavery in Egypt rather than trust in God's provision of food and his promise of a home. I pray he will allow you opportunity to live out genuine faith rather than spend your whole life living an untested, inactivated faith. I pray he will retrain your appetites away from what the world offers, and away from what you crave that will kill you, toward the food that will satisfy and sustain you as you live out your days in the wilderness of this world. I pray that even now he would fill your life with his abundant provision.

I pray that God will do his best work with the emptiness in your life as he fills you with the Holy Spirit as his presence once filled the Most Holy Place of the Tabernacle. As he does, you will no longer have to relate to him from a distance. I pray that he will make you holy as he is holy so that you can live in his presence. I pray that you will know and sense that he is with you, even within you, and that you are never alone.

I pray that God will do his best work with the emptiness in your life, as he did in Naomi's life. I pray that you will not see your emptiness as evidence that his hand has turned against you, but rather as an invitation to turn toward him. I pray that you will put yourself at the feet of the Redeemer and ask him to cover you, provide for you, and redeem you, and that he will fill your life with his saving and sustaining grace.

I pray that God will do his best work with the emptiness in your life, just as he did in Mephibosheth's life. I pray that you will see how he sought you out and brought you to himself, and that he is determined to one day restore to you what the cruelties of life have taken away. I pray that you will come to the place he has made for you at his table where he wants to share life with you day by day, now and into eternity. I pray that he will fill your life with his generous kindness in such a way that you want to extend kindness to others.

I pray that God will do his best work with the emptiness in your life as he calls you away from the broken cisterns you keep trying to drink from that don't hold the water you need to live. I pray that, like the woman at the well, you will drink the living water that will quench the thirst you have to love and be loved in return with a love that is strong enough, powerful enough, and enduring enough to exceed your expectations and desires.

I pray that God will do his best work with the emptiness in your life by providing the perspective you need for living in this world Q described to us in the book of Ecclesiastes, a world that doesn't work right. As you are joined to Christ, who is Wisdom incarnate, I pray he will help you to grasp how the ongoing disappointments of this life under the sun are turning your heart toward the life to come in the new heaven and new earth. I pray he will fill your life with meaning and purpose.

I pray that God will do his best work with the emptiness in your life, just as he did in Habakkuk's life. I pray that he will meet you in your fears about the future, giving you a song to sing as you wait for whatever comes. I pray that he will fill you with the faith to trust him with the possibility of losing everything in this life, even your own life. And I pray that he will fill you with joy in his salvation beyond this world.

As you come to Christ, our ultimate Treasure, with the posture of openhanded surrender, I pray he will work in your life and through your life in ways that gain for you treasures in heaven that cannot be taken away. I pray that he will fill your eternal future with the treasure of face-to-face relationship with him that results in endless satisfaction and joy.

I pray that the day will come when you will be able to look back over the course of your lifetime and see that again and again, God did his best work in the empty places, the desperate times, and the difficult circumstances in your life, and that he has filled you with the fullness of Christ.

BIBLIOGRAPHY

Allen, Michael. "Divine Fullness: A Dogmatic Sketch." *Reformed Faith and Practice* 1, no. 1 (2016): 5–18.

Ash, Christopher. *Teaching Ruth & Esther*. Ross-Shire, Scotland: Christian Focus, 2018.

———. *Married for God: Making Your Marriage the Best It Can Be*. Wheaton, IL: Crossway, 2016.

Bartholomew, Tuck. "Leadership and Community." Sermon, Redeemer Presbyterian Church, New York, NY, November 17, 2002.

Bewes, Richard. "Walking on Air." Sermon, All Souls Langham Place, London, June 14, 1998.

Blackham, Paul. *2 Samuel*. Book by Book. Preston, England: Biblical Frameworks, 2017.

Bloom, Jon. "The Treasure Makes All the Difference," DesiringGod. org, June 13, 2014. https://www.desiringgod.org/ articles/the-treasure-makes-all-the-difference.

Carson, D. A. *Praying with Paul: A Call to Spiritual Reformation*. Grand Rapids, MI: Baker Academic, 1992, 2014.

Duguid, Iain. *Esther & Ruth Reformed Expository Commentary*, edited by Richard D. Phillips and Philip Graham Ryken. Phillipsburg, NJ: P&R Publishing, 2005.

Eswine, Zack. *Recovering Eden: The Gospel according to Ecclesiastes.* The Gospel according to the Old Testament. Phillipsburg, NJ: P&R Publishing, 2014.

Gibson, David. *Living Life Backward: How Ecclesiastes Teaches Us to Live in Light of the End.* Wheaton, IL: Crossway, 2017.

Guthrie, Nancy. *Even Better than Eden: Nine Ways the Bible's Story Changes Everything about Your Story.* Wheaton, IL: Crossway, 2018.

———. *The Lamb of God: Seeing Jesus in Exodus, Leviticus, Numbers and Deuteronomy.* Wheaton, IL: Crossway, 2012.

———. *The Word of the Lord: Seeing Jesus in the Prophets.* Wheaton, IL: Crossway, 2014.

Helm, David. "Following the King." Sermon, Holy Trinity Church, Chicago, IL, July 20, 2013.

Jackman, David. "Trusting." Sermon, St. Helen's Bishopsgate, London, November 24, 1996.

Keller, Tim. "The Parable of the Pearl; On Priorities." Sermon, Redeemer Presbyterian Church, New York, NY, August 28, 1994.

Kelly, Ryan. "Kindness Received, Kindness Rejected." Sermon, Desert Springs Church, November 1, 2015.

Miller, Paul. *A Loving Life: In a World of Broken Relationships.* Wheaton, IL: Crossway, 2014.

O'Donnell, Douglas Sean. *Matthew: All Authority in Heaven and on Earth, Preaching the Word.* Wheaton, IL: Crossway, 2013.

Piper, John. "Jesus Came Not to Give Bread but to Be Bread." Sermon, Angola Prison, Angola, LA, November 19, 2009.

———. "The Kingdom of Heaven Is a Treasure." Sermon, Bethlehem Baptist Church, Minneapolis, MN, November 20, 2005.

Sach, Andrew. "How Long O Lord?" Sermon, St. Helen's Bishopsgate, London, August 2, 2015.

Shiner, Rory. "Chapel Service – Week 10." Sermon, Queensland Theological College, Brisbane, Australia, April 30, 2019.

Skrine, Charlie. "Eat Jesus and Live Forever." Sermon, St. Helen's Bishopsgate, London, August 10, 2014.

Shurden, Nate. "Keeping Covenant." Sermon, Cornerstone Presbyterian Church, Franklin, TN, June 12, 2016.

Sklar, Jay. "The Lord Is against Me." Sermon, Southwood Presbyterian Church, Huntsville, AL, July 9, 2006.

Smith, Colin. "The Just Shall Live by Faith." Sermon, The Orchard Evangelical Free Church, Arlington Heights, IL, December 10, 2000.

Taylor, William. "The Gift of Life." Sermon, St. Helen's Bishopsgate, London, November 6, 2012.

Tice, Rico. "I Can't Get No Satisfaction." Sermon, All Souls Langham Place, London, January 14, 2007.

―――. "Our God Is Marching On." Sermon, All Souls Langham Place, London, June 7, 1998.

Tripp, Paul. "David and Mephibosheth: For the Sake of a Friend." Sermon, Tenth Presbyterian Church, Philadelphia, PA, December 28, 2008.

Woodhouse, John. *2 Samuel Your Kingdom Come.* Preaching the Word, edited by R. Kent Hughes. Wheaton, IL: Crossway, 2015.

ABOUT THE AUTHOR

NANCY GUTHRIE teaches the Bible at her church, Cornerstone Presbyterian Church, in Franklin, Tennessee, and speaks at conferences around the country and internationally. She is currently pursuing graduate studies at Reformed Theological Seminary Global. She and her husband, David, are the cohosts of the GriefShare video series used in more than twelve thousand churches around the world, and they host Respite Retreats for couples who have faced the death of a child. Nancy is the author of numerous books and Bible studies, including *Holding On to Hope*, *The One Year Book of Hope*, and *Praying through the Bible for Your Kids*. She also hosts the *Help Me Teach the Bible* podcast at The Gospel Coalition. You can find more information about Nancy's family and ministry at www.nancyguthrie.com.

NOTES

1. You can read my story of how God met me in the loss of two of my children in my books *Holding On to Hope* (Tyndale, 2002) and *Hearing Jesus Speak into Your Sorrow* (Tyndale, 2009).

2. The previous three paragraphs include content adapted from the first chapter of my book *Even Better than Eden: Nine Ways the Bible's Story Changes Everything about Your Story* (Wheaton, IL: Crossway, 2018), 16–17. Used with permission of the publisher.

3. This idea of the Israelites looking at life through the knothole of their craving comes from Dr. Tuck Bartholomew, in his sermon, "Leadership and Community" given at Redeemer Presbyterian Church, New York, NY, November 17, 2002.

4. Parts of this section are adapted from my book *The Lamb of God: Seeing Jesus in Exodus, Leviticus, Numbers, and Deuteronomy* (Wheaton, IL: Crossway, 2012), 224–225. Used with permission of the publisher.

5. Dr. Vivek Murthy, *CBS This Morning*, October 19, 2017.

6. Jason Daley, "The U.K. Now Has a 'Minister for Loneliness.' Here's Why It Matters," Smithsonian, January 19, 2018, https://www .smithsonianmag.com/smart-news/minister-loneliness-appointed -united-kingdom-180967883/.

7. Augustine, *Confessions*, 1.1.1.

8. Peter Kreeft, *I Burned for Your Peace: Augustine's Confessions Unpacked* (San Francisco: Ignatius Press, 2016), 22.

9. "He is the God who made the world and everything in it. Since he

is Lord of heaven and earth, he doesn't live in man-made temples, and human hands can't serve his needs—for he has no needs. He himself gives life and breath to everything, and he satisfies every need" (Acts 17:24-25).

10. Exodus 40:38; 2 Chronicles 7:1; Ezekiel 10:4.

11. David Helm, untitled sermon on Ruth 3 (Holy Trinity Church, Chicago, IL, August 24, 2008).

12. This imagery of Mephibosheth falling from grace and then falling into grace is taken from Nate Shurden's sermon "Keeping Covenant," given at Cornerstone Presbyterian Church on June 12, 2016.

13. Rico Tice, "I Can't Get No Satisfaction" (sermon, All Souls Langham Place, London, England, January 14, 2007).

14. Nancy Guthrie, *Even Better than Eden: Nine Ways the Bible's Story Changes Everything about Your Story* (Crossway: Wheaton, IL, 2018), 90. Used with permission of the publisher.

15. Adapted from David Gibson, *Living Life Backward: How Ecclesiastes Teaches Us to Live in Light of the End* (Wheaton, IL: Crossway, 2018), 28.

16. Nancy Guthrie, *O Love That Will Not Let Me Go: Facing Death with Courageous Confidence in God* (Wheaton, IL: Crossway, 2011).

17. Nancy Guthrie, *The Word of the Lord: Seeing Jesus in the Prophets* (Wheaton, IL: Crossway, 2014), 153. Used with permission of the publisher.

18. Rico Tice, "Habakkuk: Our God Is Marching On" (sermon, All Souls Langham Place, London, England, June 7, 1998).

19. Colin Smith, "Faith" (sermon, The Orchard Evangelical Free Church, Arlington Heights, IL, December 10, 2000).

20. Ibid.

21. Madeline Boardman, "10 of the Most Valuable Antiques Roadshow Finds," *Entertainment Weekly*, January 9, 2017, https://ew.com/tv/antiques-roadshow-most-valuable/.

22. Thomas Chalmers, "The Expulsive Power of a New Affection" (sermon).

BY NANCY GUTHRIE

BOOKS

Holding On to Hope

The One Year® Book of Hope

*Hearing Jesus Speak
into Your Sorrow*

*When Your Family's
Lost a Loved One
(with David Guthrie)*

*What Grieving People Wish
You Knew about What Really
Helps (and What Really Hurts)*

*One Year® of Dinner
Table Devotions and
Discussion Starters*

*The One Year® Book of
Discovering Jesus in
the Old Testament*

Abundant Life in Jesus

*The One Year® Praying
through the Bible for Your Kids*

BOOKS (CONT.)

Seeing Jesus

*What Every Child Should
Know about Prayer*

BIBLE STUDIES

Hoping for Something Better

The Promised One

The Lamb of God

The Son of David

The Wisdom of God

The Word of the Lord

Even Better than Eden

*Saints and Scoundrels
in the Story of Jesus*